HOW TO MAKE MONEY OUT OF WRITING

This book is for the three ladies in my life:
Helen, Deborah and Rebecca

How to Make Money Out of Writing

The Beginning Writer's Handbook

GRAHAM R. STEVENSON

Wildwood House

Published by
Wildwood House Limited
Gower House
Croft Road
Aldershot
Hants GU11 3HR
England

Gower Publishing Company
Old Post Road
Brookfield
Vermont 05036
USA

British Library Cataloguing in Publication Data
Stevenson, Graham
How to make money out of writing : beginning writers handbook.
1. Writing
I. Title
808'.02

ISBN 0 7045 0630 0

Printed in Great Britain by
Billing & Sons Ltd, Worcester

Contents

I found writing a book very strange
because I'd never written one before.
It was like starting on Everest when
you hadn't climbed the Chilterns.

Mary Soames

Introduction

Almost anyone can write saleable short material for magazines if they know how to go about it. It doesn't necessarily take great literary talent. If you can read and write and can use a dictionary you can write for publication. The quality of your work may not be as good as others', it is true, but then not everyone can aspire to become a second Shakespeare, Dickens or Verne.

Many aspiring authors fail to set pen to paper in the misguided belief that the marketplace simply isn't open to them. Usually, this is because they are daunted by thoughts of competition from the professionals, those 'gifted' people who spend their lives writing for a living. Surely, there isn't room for part-timers too?

Well, yes, there certainly is.

What many would-be writers fail to recognize is that a high proportion of published work is penned by spare-time writers as their hobby. They, too, started with very little knowledge of the marketplace and its requirements. They had to learn their craft through hours of study and practice. Many of them came to learn, as did I, that some areas of writing are easier to master than others; indeed, some take no literary ability whatsoever.

The same can be said of markets – there are hundreds of magazines, the majority of which the general public are unaware of. And a great many of these periodicals rely on freelance contributions to keep going. These are the publications upon which the apprentice would do well to concentrate his efforts.

This book sets out to guide beginning writers towards these easier markets and simpler forms of writing so that they can see their work published in the shortest possible time. The key is learning what to write and for which market. By far the easiest market to penetrate is that of the filler.

What is a Filler?

A filler used to be a short item at the end of a feature to make up a column when the feature ran a little short of the length necessary to fill the space allocated. Although this is still true to some extent, today, a filler has become known as any short item used to fill a gap, or simply to brighten up a page that would otherwise appear as dull text. Many periodicals carry several fillers in each edition in order to lighten their image.

There are literally thousands of magazines published every month and a great many of them use fillers. You will, of course, encounter competition in this field, but it will not be as fierce as it is in the more ambitious areas.

A filler can be a fact, a joke, an anecdote, a short verse, a health hint, a puzzle, or any of a host of other items short enough to plug the odd gap. But we shall not just be discussing fillers in the traditional meaning of the word; we shall also examine all manner of short material suitable for publication – anything relatively easy to market.

We shall look at such items as: readers' letters, short articles, recipes, crossword puzzles, cartoons, short stories.

Yes, I did say short stories. I know this book is supposed to be for the inexperienced but if you know where to look, even the apprentice writer can have a good chance of seeing short fiction in print. Not in any of the national glossies, I'll grant you, but in print none the less. More of this later.

Practice

Without doubt, filler writing is the quickest way for the amateur to break into print. But becoming proficient takes practice, as does everything worth doing. Don't write a letter to the editor and sit back and wait to see it printed in your favourite weekly. The chances are it will never happen. *Every* area of the writer's market holds some competition, even if that competition is from amateurs like yourself. So write something every day, preferably two or three items.

When you have written something and you have satisfied yourself it is as polished as you can make it, post it to you chosen editor. Then forget about it and write something else. The more you write the greater your chances of success.

Always carry a notebook and jot down any interesting or amusing item you come across. Don't wait until you get home, or you will forget more ideas than you remember. You can take your pen almost anywhere, can write almost anywhere: on a train, on a bus, on the back seat of a car, in a 'plane, on a park bench, in a café, even in a lift or on an escalator.

If you can afford to, think of buying yourself a pocket tape-recorder. I use one to make a record of anything that crosses my mind while I'm driving – a worthwhile investment.

Writing as a Hobby Has its Rewards

I have been writing in my spare time for a number of years and, as part of my reward, have enjoyed regular payments for my published efforts. But to me, the arrival of the editor's acceptance letter is the greatest part of my reward. That isn't to say I would necessarily continue to write if I ceased to be paid to do so – I probably wouldn't – but the simple knowledge that my writing is worth publishing is the main incentive.

In terms of cash, filler writing can also be very profitable. Payment per thousand words for fillers can feature among some of the highest rates of pay for all forms of writing. Rates for full-length work vary greatly from one magazine to another, but typically a middle-of-the-road magazine would offer in the order of £20–50 per 1000 words. (Some magazines pay as little as £15 per 1000 words for their articles and some £100 plus, but these are the extremes of the market.)

If, on the other hand, you were to examine some outlets for readers' letters you would find £5–10 typical payment for each one published. Take *Weekend*, for example: they pay £10 for every letter they use. One, sitting on my desk as I write this, is just 29 words long. This represents a payment equivalent to £345 per 1000 words. Not bad at all.

Some magazines pay less than this, of course, but others pay more. One really exceptional payer is *Reader's Digest* which offers £100 for every letter they print under their 'Life's Like That' banner. One I have just read was 42 words long: a truly astonishing £2380 per 1000 words.

Whether you wish to write for pleasure or profit as your reward, fillers can certainly fulfil both criteria. But before you begin to tackle the better-paying markets, concentrate on the less-known ones; competition won't be so fierce.

Just a Beginning

The filler is the ideal vehicle to encourage the newcomer to write, as success can be achieved so quickly. It is possible with a reader's letter to see your work in print within a month of posting it. Fired by this prospect some people write nothing but fillers, content simply to spend their free moments writing the odd reader's letter, or a limerick maybe, perhaps taking the odd snapshot of unusual signs they have seen out shopping. A more absorbing hobby would be difficult to find. And filler writing is ideal for those who don't have a great deal of spare time.

For those who aspire to greater heights, writing short items can be a stepping-stone to more ambitious projects, teaching them application, how to research, simply how to write.

But don't be tempted to abandon fillers altogether when you decide to write your first full-length work, or it could be a very long time before you see any of your work in print again.

A novel of average length will be 50–80,000 words long. This could take perhaps a year or more to write. Once you have lovingly typed the manuscript, checked it and sent it to your chosen publisher eighteen months may have passed since you first set pen to paper. And finally, after your potential publisher has spent another three or four months having your work looked at, it may well be returned with a rejection notice. Two years may have elapsed and you will have written and submitted only one manuscript – a manuscript that at the end of the day could so easily prove unsuccessful. Not a very encouraging start.

So if you have aspirations to write a book or a novel it is a good idea to keep your hand in with fillers as well, just to keep up your morale. Remember, if you have twenty fillers out on offer you have nineteen more chances of an acceptance than if you stick to your one novel.

1 What to Write

Cuttings and Quotes

Scissors Are All You Need

The easiest route to an editorial acceptance is not by actually writing anything at all, but simply by a study of what others have written. If you can find published material to suit one of three outlets the satirical magazine *Private Eye* has to offer, you could earn yourself a cheque just for telling them about it.

Private Eye publish amusing and/or outrageous quotes attributed to women's liberationists. These are sent in by readers and are published under their 'Wimmin' banner in every issue. There are usually three quotes in each issue for which £5 is paid to the sender of each. One they used was attributed to the General Meeting notes of the University of Edinburgh. It read:

> Fighting for women's liberation cannot be separated from the fight against capitalism, and working-class men are the allies of working-class women in this struggle.
>
> The police and courts offer no help to women. Increasing police powers through calls for stiffer sentences for rapists, censorship of page three etc. means increasing power of the authorities to attack the working class.

Private Eye also pay £5 each for entries in their 'Pseuds Corner' slot. These are simply cuttings of pretentious quotes in print sent in by their readers. One, attributed to Lady Rothermere, in the *Daily Telegraph* read:

'I'm quite a serious person who thinks deeply about things,' she explained, lifting the telephone to order more Campari.

'My life is so bogged down with responsibilities that by evening I'm longing to put on a pretty dress and go out and have fun. I might appear frivolous but, really, all I care about is making other people happy.'

This is typical of the quotes used, and about five are published in each issue.

A third platform for your cuttings in *Private Eye* is their 'True Stories' spot. In each issue they use around seven true stories sent in by readers for which they pay £5 each. The following is a typical example:

Asked to name the book that he thought would be the biggest publishing success of 1988, Mr Robert Cardiff Jones of Gwynned Publishing said: 'The reissue as a paperback of the 1588 version of the Bible in Old Welsh.'

The submission of quotes does not, of course, require any literary ability at all, but it will get you into the swing of research, and get you used to seeing your name in your favourite magazines.

Miss Printz

Another possibility for cuttings is typographical errors. Many magazines run a regular feature of unintentional humour arising from misprints. *Punch* use around a dozen such items in their 'Country Life' spot every week. They pay £5 each for cuttings covering some item of news which never made it to the national press. One they used was attributed to the *Sale and Altrincham Advertiser*:

The ballet is on at the Palace Theatre – but there's no chance of a seat unless you are prepared to queue for standing tickets.

The weekly magazine for women, *Best*, uses a few howlers in print in their 'Paper Smiles' feature in every issue. £5 is paid for every one used, of which the following is typical:

The pilot said he had a vague recollection of a small boat coming towards him, and of an arm being held out. He hung on to it with clenched teeth.

The ever popular magazine *Weekend* uses unintentional humour in their column 'How's That Again?'. They use around five in every issue for which they pay £3 each. Typical of the items used, this one was attributed to the *Bognor and Chichester Guardian*:

He chose trout with almonds and a mixed salad and French fires.

Misprints are another easy way to get your name into print. All you need do is clip the item from the page and send it to your chosen publication. And with so many give-away newspapers falling through our letterboxes these days, there's a wealth of raw material at our disposal. These 'free-sheets' rely on so small a staff to produce their weekly editions that proof-reading is perhaps not all it might be. Read any issue and you are bound to find at least one misprint you could use.

What Did You Say?

Private Eye run a regular column under their 'Colemanballs' banner. The inception of this feature was inspired by the gobbledygook that occasionally spills from the lips of the well-known television personality, David Coleman. The reputation this gentleman has gained for getting his 'worms in a middle' has long been the basis of the *Eye's* comic column and has also provided sufficient volume of entries to fill four books.

Colemanballs are essentially quotes of well-known personalities obtained from radio, television and the press. There are five printed in every issue of the magazine with a £5 reward to the sender of each. One attributed to Simon Bates on Radio One read:

> He is in hospital suffering from a nervous breakdown, but no doubt he will soon be better and running around like a maniac.

And one by the man himself, David Coleman:

> He is accelerating all the time. That last lap was run in 64 seconds and the one before that in 62 seconds.

Who Said That?

Overheard snippets of conversation can often be the source of amusement. So the next time you hear something to make you smile why not share it with others and earn a fee into the bargain?

The weekly magazine *Chat* runs five short features every week under their heading 'The Things Kids Say'. These children's quotes earn £5 a time. Here is one they have used:

> My grandson came to me the other day and said:
> 'Nan, where did I come from?'
> So I said: 'Out of your mummy's tummy'.

He thought about that for a moment before the next question: 'But why did she eat me?'

Bella, the weekly for women, pays £10 each for funny overheard remarks and eyebrow-raising snatches of conversation printed in their 'Overheard' feature. This is typical of what they use:

> Woman to friend in Yorkshire shop: 'D'you know, she had the cheek to say I was looking old? Well, I said to her, you're no spring onion.'

Readers' Letters

Everyone Writes Letters

Just about everyone has written a letter at some point in their life. None may have been literary masterpieces, it is true, a brief 'thank you' to Aunt Maude at Christmas time, or a 'wish you were here' holiday postcard, but they still represent letter-writing experiences. So what better place to begin your writing career?

Composing a reader's letter is a very good way of learning to write simply and clearly, providing you with a sound grounding for more ambitious writing projects in the future.

A high proportion of magazines use readers' letters, so despite competition from aspiring amateurs like yourself, there is room for everyone. Newspapers, too, often publish readers' letters. But be careful, not all outlets pay for them. This may not be important to you at this point, of course. You may be content simply to see your name in print. But should income be a consideration, check to ensure your target market pays for the letters they print.

What Shall I Write About?

You should also undertake some market research before you commit pen to paper. Decide which magazines you would like to contribute to and buy at least three different issues of each. Study the letters pages thoroughly to identify editorial preferences. Topics covered will vary not only from the general subject-matter of the publication but will also depend upon the class of readership. A letter on the subject of patios submitted to *House and Gardens* will require a different treatment from one written to *Do-it-Yourself*.

General-interest magazines will also have different slants according to their readership and to editorial preferences. Some editors will use letters of a political nature, while others will use stories about children or the home. Some prefer the sting-in-the-tale variety, particularly if the writer is the one to be stung.

Should your resources be stretched, keep your eyes open wherever you go; undertake your research whenever the opportunity presents itself. On visits to the doctor's or dentist's waiting room take the opportunity to have a look at as many different magazines you are unfamiliar with as possible. Learn which use readers' letters, and more importantly which of them pay. Study their form and content so that you may write on similar lines. Don't just read the letters page, read everything; there might just be something among the articles to spark an idea for a letter. And don't forget to make a note of the editorial address before you return your precious research material to the pile on the table.

If, in the beginning, ideas are slow in coming, study the themes others have used. Ask yourself how *you* would have written *their* letters had you been submitting them for publication.

Other letters may just beg for a reply, either agreeing or disagreeing with their view. Or you may simply be able to add a new slant. You may see a different market for the theme used in their letter. Remember: *ideas* are not copyright. Provided you do not simply copy out a letter there is no reason why you shouldn't employ the same theme with another magazine. Try to be original though, if at all possible. There are few new ideas, but a novel slant will give your offering an edge over the field.

Ideas can come from many other sources. Observation of human behaviour will often spark off an idea, as it did for one of my letters published by the *Weekly News*:

> The introduction of a cash machine at my bank has really amused me. At one time I used to queue up for ages inside my bank at lunchtime, but now the queue is miles long outside. It's quicker to go inside where many of the cashiers are sitting idly by.

Humour is very often a best-seller – particularly when the laughter is generated at the expense of your own dignity; jokes aimed at oneself always find sympathy. Conversations overheard can provide amusing anecdotes, so keep an ear open whenever travelling on public transport. Travel can also be a good time to look out for graffiti that would be suitable subject-matter for a reader's letter. Indeed, both Roger Kilroy and Nigel Rees have between them sired numerous books on just that subject. Telephone kiosks, public toilets, bus shelters, underground stations – these and many more public places are ideal hunting grounds for graffiti raw material.

Hobbies and part-time interests can inspire letters. Many special interest magazines grace the stands: sewing, cooking, wine-making, DIY, gardening, photography, fishing, shooting . . . most hobbies have a periodical devoted to the speciality. And what about those other things you do every day? Could one of them be of interest to others? Just because they may be commonplace to you, they could well provide a yarn for a magazine and its readers. Those used stamps you save for Cancer Research could just earn you a reader's letter fee, and provide good publicity for your favourite charity into the bargain.

What appeared on television last night to incense or inspire you? Is sex and violence really getting out of hand? Is there too much (or not enough) politics, sport, comedy, documentaries? Analyse everything you watch to see if you can find a suitable subject for your favourite viewer's comment spot.

Everyone comes across the odd thing that irritates them. The toothpaste tube squeezed in the middle instead of at the end; the milkman who always leaves the bottles in the sunlight so that the milk turns sour before you arrive home to put it in the 'fridge; the newspaper pushed only halfway through the letterbox so that it gets soaked in the rain. One such niggle inspired me to write to *Titbits* and the £5 it earned smothered my irritation:

> The object of a signature on a credit card is presumably to allow the seller of goods to check it against the signature on the sales voucher. Trouble is, that cashiers rarely bother to look at either signature. Could it be that the space allowed for the signature on a credit card is so small that it bears no likeness to the usual one?

Whether or not we like to admit it, it is a fact that most of us have a bad habit of one kind or another. Again, humour can be a big asset here; if you are capable of laughing at your own silly excuses for laziness, or perhaps reasons why you shouldn't go on that diet *this* week, you probably have the makings of a winning reader's letter. If you are able to recognize and admit your shortcomings, you will find others who are the same and who will be able to identify with you.

Children do and say so many unexpected things they offer constant potential for material. And mother and baby magazines on the stands are in good supply. Outlets include *Young Mother, Parents, Under Five, Mother & Baby, Mother*. All of these magazines print and pay for readers' letters. Not all are humorous of course, far from it, but those that raise a smile are probably easier to come by. Observation of my own daughter inspired me to write this:

> My two year old daughter pointed to one of our feathered friends sitting on the lawn and said: 'Look, there's a blackbird over there'. 'That's a robin, dear,' I advised her. 'It's a blackbird called Robin,' was her assured response.

Animals and pets can be the source of much inspiration. Anything from the usual mongrel dog to the more exotic boa constrictor. Does anyone in your neighbourhood keep unusual pets? And have they caused any incident worthy of note? What amusing antics do your own pets get up to? Esther Rantzen made quite a feature out of a dog that could apparently say 'sausages', on her *That's Life* television programme. If your pet can do unusual tricks there must be at least a reader's letter in it.

The broad outline of ideas we have so far covered just scratches the surface of potential ideas. The potential for readers' letters is literally endless. A couple of moments' thought will reveal many more basic topics to draw from: Motoring experiences (don't we motorists have them every day?), sport, your most embarrassing moment, how things have changed over the years, what happened on your holiday; at work, at school, shopping, cooking, bathing, walking, shooting, writing . . . You can never reach the end of potential subjects.

One source of ideas you could always be working at is your ideas book. By now you should be carrying a notebook wherever you go, and as soon as something interesting comes to your notice you should be jotting it down. Sift through your notes until you find something you can slant to the magazine of your choice. Write it up, and send it out. Then ask yourself if your letter could be rewritten for another market. Your ideas book needn't be anything fancy. Anything will do. My current one is an out-of-date desk diary.

Sometimes an editor will provide the subject-matter for a letter and will invite readers' views on a specific subject. Very often this request will have been inspired by thoughts expressed in a current reader's letter. This can happen when the original letter expresses views which were particularly controversial. If you respond, your chances of an acceptance are bound to be better than a letter written on any other subject.

Respond also not just to other readers' letters, but try to think of an interesting comment to make on one of the features in the current issue. This could be criticism, praise or an additional idea or viewpoint. This is particularly a good slant if you can provide an anecdote from your own experience of the issue in question.

Letters don't have to be your own true opinion; the object of the exercise is to get published. Often you may have more chance of success if you are outspoken. You may squirm when you write your letter, but no one need know it was you who wrote it if you use the cover of a pseudonym. Then your friends, or perhaps more importantly, your boss, won't be pointing a finger at you saying how outrageous your views are.

The adoption of a *nom-de-plume* will also allow you to have more out on offer at any one time than if you were to use just your real name. You can write to the same market using different names to enhance your chances of an acceptance. But if you use longhand be careful to disguise your handwriting; you wouldn't want your multiple submissions spotted by some eagle-eye who notices letters from apparently different people in the same hand. That might not go down too well.

The use of pen-names also allows you to identify which of your letters has been accepted. This is essential if you haven't had a chance to see it in print as it ensures you will be able to send those letters that do not find favour to another market. Limit the use of a particular group of names to one particular magazine so that when the editorial cheque arrives it will be addressed to a name unique to a particular letter.

Acceptance cheques made out to your pen-names won't present a problem. Simply endorse them on the back in the name of the payee before paying them into your bank account in the usual way.

We said earlier that themes cannot in themselves be protected by copyright. But ensure you never put yourself in a position where you could be accused of plagiarism. Do not copy verbatim. Ideas may be in short supply but *never* use someone else's work as your own. Quite apart from the ethics of the matter, the chances are you would be found out. Readers often take several similar magazines regularly, and one of them would be bound to spot your plagiarism. When they did, it is highly likely a letter or two of complaint would find their way to the editor. And that would be your letter-writing career with that particular market well and truly over. Again, this doesn't mean you shouldn't use the same theme over and over again. Re-slant your ideas to suit several different markets. Make the most of your ideas.

If, after all this, you still can't come up with anything, take a look at Chapter 2 where we look at further subject ideas as well as devices to bring them out into the open.

Which Approach?

Another point to bear in mind when selecting a market is style. Letters published in one magazine may be light-hearted or humorous, others serious, and some told in anger. As we said a while ago, there will usually be a pattern for you to follow. Ask yourself some fundamental questions. How many words were used in the average sentence? How many paragraphs were there in each letter? Were the words short and simple, or long and sophisticated?

It is also important to study the length of letters already published. Most magazines have a minimum and maximum number of words they are willing to accept. Letters can vary in length from just a few words to 150, and sometimes a great deal more. Letters printed in *The News of the World* can consist of as few as a dozen words or even less, whereas *Weekend* often publish letters of 150 words or more.

One of my letters published in *Review* simply read:

> I saw this slogan scrawled in the dirt of a van: 'Don't clean me – plant something'.

Just sixteen words, but it suited the length limits of the market so it earned me a couple of pounds. If your letter is not within the publisher's length limits it will never see the news-stands. Stick to the right number of words and never use padding: quite the reverse – weed out all unnecessary words. What some take 100 words to say, others say in ten. And those who say it in ten stand a better chance of acceptance.

Writing style is a very individual thing, but your letters should flow easily. As a general principle though, particularly when writing for those magazines with a readership from the lower-income group, you should not be *too* professional. Always remember your letters should appear as though they have arisen from an interest in a particular subject, or in a particular magazine, and not with the object of making a profit.

One of the first rules for writing letters for publication, or anything else for that matter, is to forget efforts to recall the grammatical English you were taught at school. And this should apply no matter to what level of publication your letter is aimed. Your use of English should be simple and straightforward in order to achieve an easy, readable style.

One of the first letters I ever sent to a magazine appeared in *Weekend*. It read:

> Why do we have to mimic the Americans so often?Are we incapable of maintaining our own identity? Legislation first introduced in America, from women's rights to seat belts, may be all very laudable here too, but there has to be a limit to what we copy. The introduction of the American-style 'wailing' sirens on to police cars is very irritating because they are so loud. How long will it be before our police start to tote six shooters, wear stetson hats and have shiny stars pinned to their chests?

In this example the first sentence could have read: 'It is difficult to understand why the British have to copy the Americans so often.' A lot of people would have written it that way. My advice is not to use such a style. Avoid the passive style of writing; be personal. When people talk they use straightforward language. If you write the way you talk your work will probably sound right. Read it aloud. If there are no lumps and bumps, no strangulation of the tongue, the chances are it's OK.

Remember, too, that people in everyday life often use bad grammar. And this can be reflected in the readers' letters pages of the lower quality magazines. In many cases letters are written by people of a low intellect. This doesn't matter of course, as part of the charm of the letters is that readers can identify with them. They can often relate to others' everyday experiences because they recognize them as similar to their own.

In the better quality markets you will need to be more discerning in your approach. It is all a question of market research.

Have you ever considered the use of dialogue in your letters? It can often be put to good use when handled properly. Go back over the example letter to the mother and baby market we used earlier. Its very succinctness comes from its use of dialogue. I challenge you to rewrite it in narrative form to better effect.

Whatever you write, try to give your composition an eye-catching lead. A crisp opening sentence will entice the editor to read on. If he does, it's likely he'll use your letter. A simple hook device is the use of a question. Usually, the reader will go on in order to find the answer.

Whether or not you type your letters, always keep a carbon copy. If your letters are handwritten use a ball-point pen that will produce a good copy. This way you will have a permanent record of what you have offered and to whom.

And don't forget your name and address. Elementary you may think, but letters do find their way into print followed by a plea from the editor for the author to contact the magazine with their name and address so that their prize can be awarded.

Editors receive hundreds of submissions every week, and they can use only a small proportion. If in three months or so your letter has not met with success, do not lose heart, sent it somewhere else. But before you do, read it critically. Approaching it with fresh eyes, as you will be for the first time in three months, you may find you can tidy it up a little. Now send it out again.

Whatever you do, do not write to the editor asking if your letter is going to be used. That's just asking to be put on the nuisance list. Be realistic; you haven't written a novel, simply a reader's letter. It may be important to you, but to an editor your letter is just one of thousands sent in each year.

Talking of eye-catching leads; do the magazines you propose to write for give their letters headings? Many do. In general, these will be short and punchy. Capitalize on this fact by trying to emulate the style of those already in print. If you can save an editor the task of selecting a heading you may just give your offering the edge it needs to succeed.

Another winning gimmick can be the use of rhyme. Many people adopt the same straightforward approach to letters to the editor as they do to letters to their bank manager. If you can shake convention to use rhyme you could have yourself a winner. One example I read in *Family Circle* went:

> Some people in winter are prone to freeze,
> While others sweat and smother,
> And by some tricky quirk of fate,
> They marry one another.

The use of rhyme in this instance won its composer a fiver.

Another advantage of beginning your writing career with readers' letters is that it is not necessary to have them typed. But ensure your handwriting can be easily read. Editors are human, and if your writing is difficult to read they may well pass yours over in favour of something more legible.

Fillers and Things

Anecdotes

Most of us have scores of amusing and interesting things happen to us throughout our lives. If we can recognize and recall them they can be turned into profitable fillers.

The main requirement for this type of item is to be succinct and amusing.

Think about the people you know. Do any of them have names to suit their occupations? Take the lecturer at the Spiro Institute of Education, for example, who offers courses on the history of Jewish food. Her name is Mrs Bacon. Or the woman who has written a book on the subject of tarantulas, and has 70 in her home at Radlett, Herts. Her name is Mrs Ann Webb.

Our everyday lives are filled with potential material. Overheard snippets of conversation can produce many a laugh – particularly where children are concerned. I recall an incident in our back garden one summer when we had friends over for a barbecue. 'Where's Pete?' asked one of them. 'Over there', replied my two-year-old daughter as she pointed to an area where no one stood. 'Where?' repeated my friend. 'There', insisted my indignant daughter, as she trotted over to a bag of Irish moss peat.

Another area of unintentional humour to inspire the giggles in me is inaccurate translation or bad spelling. Like the sign outside the Greek restaurant which read 'WE SPEKE THE PERFEKT INGLISH'. Or Le Café de Paris, Brighton, offering, 'Traditional French Cousine'. The first restaurant into cannibalism, no doubt!

Have you ever been on jury service? The courts can produce some hilarious moments of unintentional humour. When I was at Westminster quarter sessions I saw a roughly dressed fellow leaning against the jury room door. When he noticed me eyeing him suspiciously he hooked his thumbs under his braces, threw his head back, and said in slurred speech: 'I'm the star witness for the defence.' He then giggled and fell to the floor. The defence, it seems, didn't have a leg to stand on!

Moments like these can all be a source of anecdotal fillers.

The Countryman, the quarterly magazine for country lovers, uses the occasional amusing incident in its 240 pages. The reward for these starts at around £30 per 1000 words. This example filled a gap at the end of one article:

In the days when Knighton was the county town of what was then Radnorshire and still on the circuit, the local police sergeant was called upon to give evidence.

Prosecuting counsel: 'You are Sergeant H?'
Sergeant: 'High ham.'
Judge: 'Ho.'

Another quarterly magazine devoted to country matters is *Evergreen*. They use a relatively large number of anecdotes in each issue. For those printed in their 'Scrap Book' slot, compilers receive a pack of Evergreen playing cards produced especially for the magazine by Waddington. For the senders of amusing cameos used elsewhere the reward is at the rate of £10 per 1000 words. This one appeared in the 'Scrap Book' column:

In Swansea there is a well-known firm of solicitors W. G. Christian and Sons. A letter was sent to them from overseas addressed simply 'W. G. Christian, South Wales'. It eventually arrived at their office with a note from the Post Office attached which read: 'No Christians in Cardiff, try Swansea.'

If you have a true story from your own experience showing the funny side of everyday life, 'Life's Like That' in *Reader's Digest* could be your target. Your tale will have to be exceptionally good to make this level of market, but if it does the rewards are high: £100 for every one published. This shows the kind of thing they use:

My daughter was on her way to visit me wearing a very smart, shocking-pink trouser-suit. At the station ticket-office she said, 'Do I change for Broadstairs?' Back came the immediate reply: 'No, they all dress like that down there.'

Stranger Than Fiction

A variation of the anecdote theme is the use of unusual facts. And research material for these is in abundance at any local library. Encyclopedias, factfinders and world record-type books are simply bursting with information ready to be converted into interesting and profitable fillers.

Titbits use filler items of up to 100 words, some of which are interesting or humorous facts. These items earn £8 per time.

The *Sunday Post* use them too to fill the odd gap. One they used went:

Lothian Regional Council have set up a special Women's Unit because 56 per cent of their full-time staff and 96.2 per cent of their part-time staff are women.

> Now all that's needed is a unit to look after the interests of the minority among council employees – men!

One item used in *Celebrity* read:

> After the age of 20 your brain begins to shrink. Its weight reduces by one gram annually.

The contributor of this item was no doubt well rewarded for his trouble as *Celebrity* pays at the rate of £75 per 1000 words. And they use around ten such fillers in each issue.

To get you started, perhaps you could find a market for one of these:

- At birth we have about 350 bones, but as we grow some knit together to become 209 when we finally become adult.
- The average heart beats 100,000 times every day.
- The world record for blowing smoke rings on one pull of a cigarette is 175 rings.
- The longest railway tunnel in the world is the Seikan in Japan. It is over 33 miles long.
- John Creasey wrote 564 books under 13 pen names and received 743 rejection slips.

The last item here should give heart to the aspiring author – established writers also have manuscripts rejected at one time or another just like anyone else.

News Items

There are over 900 'give-away' newspaper titles delivered throughout Britain every week. Many of these rely on their readers for a proportion of their copy.

If you or your family are involved in charity work you could do yourself, as well as your pet hobby-horse, a favour by offering their events as news stories to your local rag: NSPCC fund-raising activities, help senior citizens beat the winter campaign, your local Round Table or fête – all could be written up to good effect without too much literary talent.

A watch on your local high street can offer opportunities. A write-up on a new store being opened by a celebrity, for example, will have reader appeal. Well-known personalities always draw the crowds – that's precisely why they are there. And if you are handy with a camera so much the better; a photograph will always add pulling-power.

Births and weddings involving local well-known families always make good copy. And on a more sombre note, the death of a local celebrity will draw reader attention. A tribute could provide a compelling story.

Anything newsworthy that may have been missed by the small staff of the 'freebies' is always worth pursuing. But be warned: not all of these will offer to pay for submission. If this is important to you it would be as well to clear the point with your target editor first.

If payment (either the amount or at all) is required, you would be better off approaching your local paid-for weekly paper. Most of these will offer NUJ rates (currently the minimum is £6.80 up to 100 words and £6.40 per 100 thereafter) but check first. Competition will be stiffer here, of course, as these journals will employ their own staff writers. Try it and see. If you fail, you may just be able to squeeze something out of one of the freebies.

Ultimately, of course, there are the nationals. But unless you are a professional journalist, backed-up by an editorial desk to send you out on assignment, the chances are that good news stories will come your way only by pure chance. So if you happen across something, don't let the moment slip away; act quickly to sell your story. If you delay, someone else who hears of it may beat you to the cheque in the eager editor's hand. Use the 'phone to get your story in. If you take or send it you may have lost the lead.

Ensure you give your name and address clearly – you are unknown to them, so spell it out. Confirm any deal in writing. Almost certainly they'll check out your story with one of their staff and will write the copy in-house. But if they do use your own words the national press will usually pay NUJ rates (currently the minimum rate for the dailies £8.74 per 100 words).

Newsworthy stories are easy to spot: disasters in any form; flood, fire, violence, death, destruction, blood, drugs – all these sell well, particularly if you are lucky enough to stumble across a scoop. Editors are nearly always busy, but they are also business people. If you have something exciting to sell, they will listen. And if what you have to offer is extra exciting they'll pay way in excess of the NUJ rate.

Household Hints

Throughout our lives we often find shortcuts to lighten the load of our daily chores. So capitalize on what life has taught you by writing down your short-cut ideas and sending them off to magazines. Many of them are prepared to pay for such hints.

We all have them. It is just a question of identifying them. Think about that short-cut to washing up; or the trick you have to ease the burden of gardening; perhaps the system you've devised to speed up cutting the lawn. Such tips can be written up into saleable material. No matter how simple your idea, if it works for you, if it saves you time, effort or money, it will be of value to others.

As you go through your daily routine, be continually alert to identify your own short-cuts. Some you may have used so many times you have almost forgotten they actually are time-savers. Make a list of your everyday chores; examine each to determine ways you have found to make life easier – or better still, how to save money. What do you most hate doing? Whatever it is, the chances are you've found a short-cut to make it more bearable. Think also of that annoying problem that's just cropped up. Once you've devised a system to overcome it let an editor know about it. He may just be happy to pay you for it.

Many popular magazines pay for household tips. *Family Circle* print around eight hints in each issue under the headline 'Take A Tip'. Each one published earns £5. Here is an example of one they have used:

> If your suede shoes need a clean but you've run out of suede cleaner, simply boil the kettle and brush them in the steam. Pack toes with newspaper to make sure they keep their shape while they dry.

Bella also use seven or eight hints for which they offer £5 each. They say, 'Share your household tips with us, the hints and short-cuts that save you time and money and make life that little bit easier.' One example from this 'How to From you' slot read:

> *Polishing Silver.* Out of polish? Toothpaste makes a convenient substitute. Scrub with a rag and rinse thoroughly with cold water.

Best use 'Tips, Tricks And Good Ideas', and they pay £5 for each of the ten or so used every week. Here's one:

> Recycle screw-top jars to use in the kitchen for storing fruit, nuts, spices, etc. or in the garage for screws, nuts and bolts. Simply pierce the lid of the jar with a bradawl and attach it to the underside of the shelf with an ordinary wood screw. Fill the jar with goodies and twist into place on the lid.

The *Weekly News* says: 'How about sharing your favourite handy hints with other readers?' They use about five 'Top Tips' in each issue. There is £5 for the best one £3 for the rest. Here is one that made runner-up:

> Here's a handy tip for knitters. Always place the descriptive band inside the centre of your ball of wool so that it's there for reference if renewal is needed.

Chat may just be interested in one of 'Your Top Tips'. Five appear in each issue for which the reward is £5 each. One of their readers advises:

> After cleaning a paintbrush with emulsion paint on it, place it in a plastic bag with an elastic band around the handle. It stops the bristles drying hard and falling out.

None of the hints quoted here are earth-shattering revelations, but all are useful tips which have earned their authors a small fee. Here are a few short-cuts my family came up with when I asked them; perhaps you could find a home for one of them:

- To reduce the time you have to spend in the kitchen, make meals for a month and freeze them in daily portions.
- To save washing tights by hand, put them into a pillowcase and they can be safely washed in your machine.
- Sprigs of mint frozen in ice-cubes will make summer drinks that much more refreshing.
- A plastic bottle filled with crushed ice will keep your food shopping fresh during hot weather.

Recipes

Do your friends ask for your recipes after they've sampled your cooking? If they do you are probably onto a winner. If you like good food and enjoy cooking, your recipes can be used to your advantage. Write them up and send them out; many magazines use readers' recipes.

You mustn't just copy a recipe from a cookbook, of course. It has to be your own invention. That isn't to say you shouldn't experiment with published recipes to arrive at your own version of them.

Whatever you cook, ask yourself if you could write it up to suit one of the popular weeklies. And always be on the lookout for something new. Collect recipes when you are abroad on holiday. Add this ingredient, delete that one: turn them into your own specialities.

Your culinary favourites won't take great literary skill to write. A list of ingredients with weights and measures, and a step-by-step description of what to do (mixing and cooking instructions in the correct sequence). Include preparation and cooking times and the number of people the dish will serve.

And remember that market research is as important a consideration for recipes as it is with any other area of freelance writing. Check to see what has been used before. If a sausage casserole has just been printed it is unlikely that a similar dish will be used for some considerable time. So try something else.

Analyse what types of meal are covered by your target magazine. Are main courses the usual choice, or are exotic desserts favoured?

Remember also the income group of the typical readership. If they are of the lower-income group, economy meals may well be preferred. Alternatively, they may be those who could well afford a gourmet treat.

Many women's magazines cater for the slimmer; are diet meals the norm?

What of the ethnic readership? French, Greek, Italian, Chinese.

Examine also the content and layout of the established recipe market. Are the costs of ingredients included? The cost per person?

A great many magazines use recipes by regular contributors or house writers, so check before submitting yours. Should you aim for an outlet which is not an obvious 'reader's recipe' slot, ensure you include a brief note to the editor to say why you are qualified to write on the subject. Include your many years of cooking as a hobby, perhaps the courses you have attended. If you have a certificate or two, so much the better.

Presentation, too, counts just as much in this area of writing as any other. Ensure the layout of your recipe is exactly as others have been presented before. Make your copy clean and neat.

Chat publish a reader's recipe in every issue and award £10 for it. One they published was named after its creator, Mrs. J. Rooker: it was called Rooker's Porker. This listed twelve ingredients together with a descriptive method of 85 words. The cost per person was given, as were the preparation and cooking times.

'Rural Recipes' are occasionally published in *Evergreen*, for which they make a small payment. One they used was for Welsh cakes. This listed eight ingredients with a description of 65 words.

Informative Fillers

Informative fillers are simply articles in miniature. They are usually between 50 and 500 words long and appear in the majority of periodicals. Their subject-matter can be as varied as any full-length article, and will depend upon the editorial style of the publication in question.

When preparing for this kind of filler it is usually best to stick to what you know best. Write about your interests, your hobby, or your job. This will keep the amount of research you need to undertake down to a minimum. Also, if you write about those things familiar to you, your writing will hold more facts and figures which will mean your article will be more convincing and therefore more interesting.

Don't worry too much about writing technique at this stage, concentrate on presenting your information as simple statements; let the facts speak for themselves. Provided your information is presented simply and lucidly your piece is likely to be readable.

The informative filler can be the springboard to more ambitious projects. Once you have become proficient at writing and selling such items you may wish to progress into the production of full-length articles. More of this later.

One of the simplest avenues into the filler market is via one of the many magazines inviting stories from their readers. The *Weekly News* publish around four mini-articles in the 'Meet The Family' slot each week. These are usually between 250 and 300 words. Each has a headline, as well as one or two subheadings to break up the text. The magazine invites: 'Moving stories about the unusual and amusing events that add drama, humour and excitement to everyday family life'. A typical issue contained these themes:

- The story of a housewife who contacted the Fire Brigade because she left her heated rollers switched on when she went on holiday.
- How a young baby was saved from being crushed, by the hood of his pram, when a ceiling collapsed.
- A family on holiday in Corfu adopt a stray dog who is blind in one eye.
- An accident-prone boy who has broken his arm seven times over the years, now sets the garden alight.

The first of these stories was awarded £10, and the others £5.

Each week *Bella* print three personal pieces submitted by readers in their 'Precious Moments' slot. These are generally on the subject of family life where readers share touching, tender or joyous moments from the wonder of their lives. These are stories of around 250 words. Each of these fillers has a headline and is accompanied by a photograph of the personality/ies forming the subject of the piece. Payment for these is £25. A typical issue contained:

- Childhood sweethearts reunite after a sixty-year separation.
- A caring husband tackles a freezing blizzard to see his wife in hospital.
- Childhood sweethearts part after a misunderstanding but meet again, eventually to see their 38th wedding anniversary.

Once you have gained experience with these markets you can think of writing and submitting informative fillers to a more varied selection of editors.

The quarterly magazine *Evergreen* is an ideal target market for informative fillers of around 100 words or more. All material used is of a country flavour covering such areas as Britain's famous people (and infamous characters), its natural beauty, towns and villages, history, traditions, odd customs, legends, folklore, surviving crafts, etc. Payment is at the rate of £10 per 1000 words except for items used in their 'Scrap Book' corner where a prize of a pack of Evergreen playing cards is awarded to each contribution used.

Further up the market ladder still we see the national weekly glossies.

Celebrity uses a dozen or so mini-articles of up to 500 words each in every issue. Payment is good – their standard rate for features is £75 per 1000 words. The magazine is aimed at a down-market readership (both men and women) aged between 18 and 45.

Titbits use around ten short pieces in each edition. Their preferred length is 100 words, for which the pay is at the rate of £80 per 1000. Still in tabloid format this magazine is aimed at a wide readership aged between 15 and 65.

Chat is also a tabloid-style magazine aimed at women (although they do have some male readers). They use a number of informative fillers of varying lengths, but this is said to be one of the harder markets to penetrate. Rates of pay depend upon merit.

Rhythm and Rhyme

Many periodicals use verse to fill the odd corner. And the use of the term 'verse' and not 'poetry' is quite deliberate. The *Concise Oxford Dictionary* defines a poem as: 'elevated composition in prose or verse'. The important word here is 'elevated'. The verse I propose to discuss would probably not be 'elevated' enough to warrant the description of poetry.

The production of serious poetry usually follows a great deal of study, for it is a complex subject and not for the beginner who wishes to see their work in print.

The market for published poetry is extremely small. The main outlet is the small press magazines devoted to its exposure. Some of the more fortunate of these are subsidized by the Arts Council, but a great many more are produced by enthusiastic poets themselves. The majority of these are produced on a shoestring budget which, in the majority of cases, cannot stretch to the payment of fees to contributors. The competition for space in these specialist magazines is fierce. The poetry magazine *Outposts*, for example, receives 83,000 poems a year, but can only print about 120. This is just one in 700 – less than one-fifth of one per cent. So, if you wish to become a serious poet, I suggest you make a separate study of the art.

Less serious-minded scribes shouldn't be put off by these facts. Outlets still exist for those who know a little of the art. It doesn't have to take a dedicated poet to produce saleable verse. Indeed, little of the technicalities need be known at all. As one anonymous child said in an essay: 'Poetry is the stuff in books that doesn't quite reach the margins.' Well, perhaps that is *too* simplistic, but it's not far off.

The first thing to consider is subject-matter. What can you write about?

The answer to that is: just about anything, although it will tend to develop easier in your mind if it is something close to your heart. Will the boss give you a rise this week? Isn't the garden lovely following rain? Nothing is more uplifting than a child's laughter. Anything can be used as the subject-matter for verse.

Once you have your idea you will need to give it form. Just as the granite block lacks form prior to blows from the sculptor's chisel, so words in themselves lack form; it is for the writer to give them that. There are many moulds used in poetry, including blank and free verse. Rhymes are simply words that sound alike, or have a close similarity of sound in words of final syllables. One point of view says that if it doesn't rhyme, it isn't poetry; another that rhyming verse is outdated. Either way, our object is to expose the easier avenues into print and undoubtedly the main market is for rhyming verse.

There is a multitude of rhyming verse forms. The limerick, for example, is a five-lined humorous or nonsensical poem, where the first, second and fifth lines rhyme with each other, as do the third and fourth. Here is one of mine which appeared in *Revue*:

A wizened old man from Kent,
Had a back that was exceedingly bent.
When his feet point South,
To the North did his mouth,
So instead of coming he went.

The most common rhyming form is where lines rhyme in pairs: the first with the second, the third with the fourth, etc. But there are many other variations.

Not all lines need to rhyme to achieve a pleasing sound. If we represent similar sounding line endings with a letter of the alphabet, we can see some typical combinations below:

a	a	a	a
a	b	b	a
b	a	c	b
	b	b	c
c			c
c			b
b	c	d	
	d	e	
	c	f	
d	d	e	d
d			e
b			f
			f
			e

It doesn't take a detailed study of published verse to be able to concoct a multitude of variations on the above theme. An invaluable asset here is a rhyming dictionary. This will normally include many more rhyming words than we are conscious of, and will often overcome sticky situations when a rhyme will not readily come to mind. (See Chapter 8 for recommended reference books.)

Your verse will also need rhythm. We won't get bogged down with such technical terms as trochaic, dactylic, iambic, anapaestic (all rhythm patterns), suffice it to say that your verse needs a beat, a regular occurrence and cessation of sounds. If you think of your poem as a piece of music you are halfway there. Imagine your music teacher at school trying to convey the beat of the waltz: ONE, two, three, ONE, two, three, ONE, two, three . . .

Once you have your subject, rhythm and rhyme consolidated into a poem you will need to find a home for it.

The quarterly magazine *The Countryman* usually uses two poems in each edition. These vary in length from a couple of lines to a two-page spread. Style also varies, but the majority are non-humorous. Payment is according to length but is quite good; their minimum rate for articles, for example, is £40 per 1000 words.

Another quarterly, *Evergreen,* also uses poetry; some twenty in each issue. Again, style varies and the editor states that poetry should be meaningful rather than 'clever'. A study of the magazine is, as always, advised to gain its flavour. The verse used is usually short. Payment is £2 per poem.

Moving up the market scale to the weeklies, *Chat* print a poem in their 'Poet's Corner' feature, and pay £10. Typically, these poems are around ten lines each, and always carry a title. The editor declares: 'All poems must be original, not copied, to include some details about yourself.'

Another potential market the writer of verse should consider is that of greetings cards. There are over 300 greetings and publishing houses in the UK many of whom accept freelance material. But be careful, not all of them do. Check first.

Largely, the verse used in this market is short – rarely more than eight lines – and the language is simple, never over-sentimental or sickly.

You'll never get rich from this market: typically payment is £1 per line – and that for the copyright. While the watchword in general in writing circles is 'think hard before selling copyright', you'll rarely be able to do otherwise when dealing with card publishers. They won't deal any other way.

Best Jests

Jokes

Humour is an elusive quality that is difficult to define; what causes some to roar with laughter elicits only a yawn from others.

It isn't easy to be funny. And there is little worse than bad humour – unless of course, it is intentionally so: corn still holds its place in the market. But if you have what it takes your work will easily find a buyer.

Writing humour at a desk is perhaps not the best place to finalize your thoughts, for, as Michael Crawford once said, 'A joke isn't a joke until someone laughs.' How can you know what you have written is funny until someone has laughed at it? You cannot. The best bet is to try out your humour on live subjects before you finish your manuscript.

Humour, like clothes, goes in fashions, so it is important to keep up to date with current trends. Keep a cuttings file; anything that raises a smile in you could be used as the basis of one of your humour submissions.

Be observant and try to see the humour in everyday situations around you. Humour can spring from ideas and situations when you least expect them, so be alert and make a written note of them as they arise.

There is no set formula for successful humour, but it must be crisply written. Puns, quips, epigrams are good starting points.

A quip is a clever or witty remark; a good word to sum it up would be 'wisecrack'. Quips are often used on the daily tear-off sheets of desk-top calendars. Example: 'The majority of us have a good aim in life, but a number simply don't know when to pull the trigger.'

A pun is the use of a word or words having several meanings, or of two words having the same sound but different meanings, in order to create humour. Example; 'Observing two housewives in heated debate across a garden fence, a man remarked that they would never agree because they were arguing from different premises.'

An epigram is a pungent saying; a biting or pointed remark. It is a lesson of life told in just a few words. Example: 'If you want to prevent the 'phone ringing while you read *War and Peace*, ask your wife to 'phone a friend.'

This form of humour can be written up to suit a number of national markets as some of the following examples demonstrate.

Four 'Laughter Lines' of around three to four lines each are printed in each issue of *Best*. These earn £5 each. Here is one they have used:

Where do gnomes go to recover from illness?
An elf clinic.

Evergreen use the odd humorous item in each issue, often in their 'Scrap Book' collection. Here is a humorous definition they have published:

A Celebrity: A person who works hard to become famous and then wears dark glasses to avoid being recognized.

'Tail Corn' first appeared in *The Countryman* in 1946, and one or two are still used to this day to fill in at the end of an article. Here is one they used, which is typical:

Tail Corn. One of my neighbours, who was collecting for the village church restoration fund, to us: 'My husband says he's not contributing anymore. He says that church tower is nothing but a bottomless pit.'

Bella invites its readers to 'Tell Us a Joke'. There are usually three in each issue, all of which earn £5. Typically these are 30–50 words long. Example:

Feeling lonely, a diner asked her waiter for a 'steak and kidney pie . . . and a kind word'. When her food arrived, she inquired, 'And the kind word?' The waiter whispered, 'Don't eat the pie.'

The first of my jokes to be published appeared in *The Weekly News*. They continue to use half a dozen or so three- or four-line jokes in each issue. They say: 'Everyone enjoys a chuckle, so let's have your favourite joke for *Laugh Lines*.' Each one published earns £2. This is typical of those printed:

Ken – 'Can you skate?
Ben – 'I don't know – I can never stand up long enough to find out!'

An unusual approach to humour can be found in each issue of *Punch*. £25 is paid for the best new caption to two cartoons printed each week. These are usually nineteenth century or early twentieth-century reprints whose captions have been omitted. It is up to the author-reader to submit a witty interpretation of what is being said by those portrayed in the picture.

Cartoons

Some of you may already have a talent for drawing, but may have never considered the possibility of using it to produce commercial cartoons. Or perhaps you have considered the idea but haven't the

Figure 1

vaguest notion of how to go about submitting them to magazines and newspapers. Well, this side of the business isn't too difficult, as we shall see.

But those of you who currently don't draw needn't skip this section; you don't have to be Giles to get published. Cartoons these days are often very simple drawings depicting just one or two characters in humble surroundings. These are drawn in line with no tone or half-tones – black only is used for contrast. It is, after all, the idea behind the cartoon that is important.

Don't become overawed by all the materials and equipment you can see in art shops. It isn't necessary to get kitted out with a light box, dozens of pallets, scores of pens, brushes and inks, expensive Bristol board. All you need are just a few basic materials – pencil, eraser, pen, ink and a brush and/or fibre-tipped pens, some cartridge paper (80g photocopying is good enough), and flat surface to work on. If you use a fibre-tipped pen though, do keep a watchful eye on its effectiveness for they tend to deteriorate with use. Points can break down and become ragged, and ink density eventually fades.

The majority of cartoons feature people as their main focus. Some cartoonists rely heavily upon the artistic treatment of the characters they create in order to convey humour. The fat, sweating, city gent running for his bus; the woman bending in the breeze; the macho, broad-shouldered sergeant-major bellowing at his troops. If you have the artistic ability, fine, but if not, don't worry. You can still produce acceptable human figures without it. Begin by drawing matchstick figures to obtain proportion (Figure 1). Work on these basic forms until you can produce full figures in different attitudes.

While your drawings need only be in simple line, there are times when a sense of perspective will help to develop a scene. You won't always need it but as it is relatively simple to conjure up we'll say a word or two about it here.

As objects get further away they appear to diminish in the eye of the observer. Trees on the horizon seem minute in comparison with the tree under which one is standing. The same principle applies to a lesser degree with items placed just a few feet away. The edge of

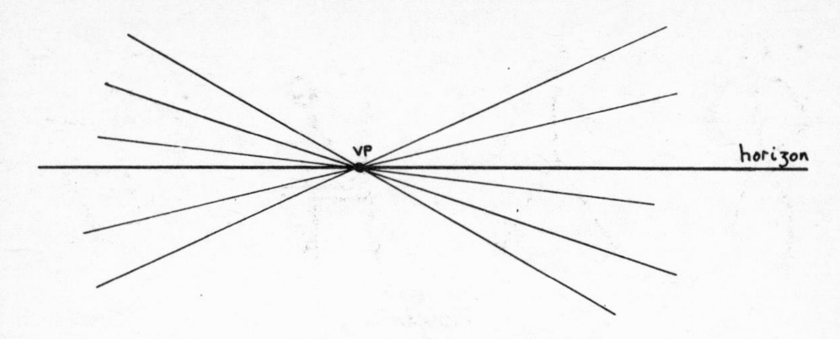

Figure 2

the table nearest you will appear slightly longer than that edge furthest away.

As a general principle, the horizon is that plane to which the eye relates all things in drawing. All objects will diminish in size as they approach a point on the horizon.

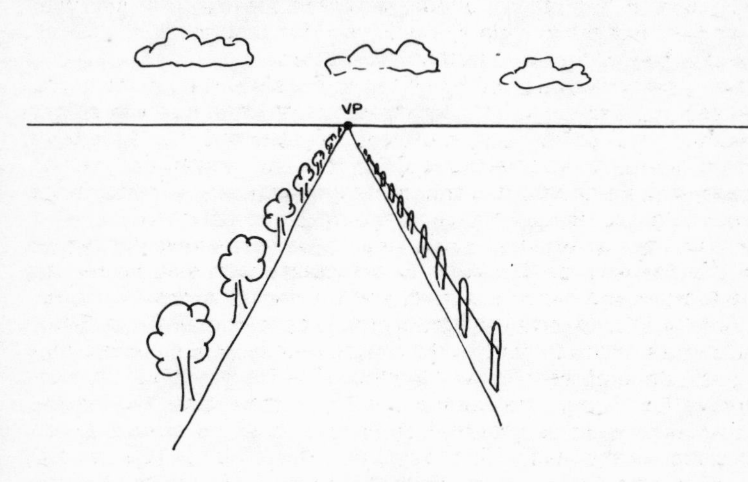

Figure 3

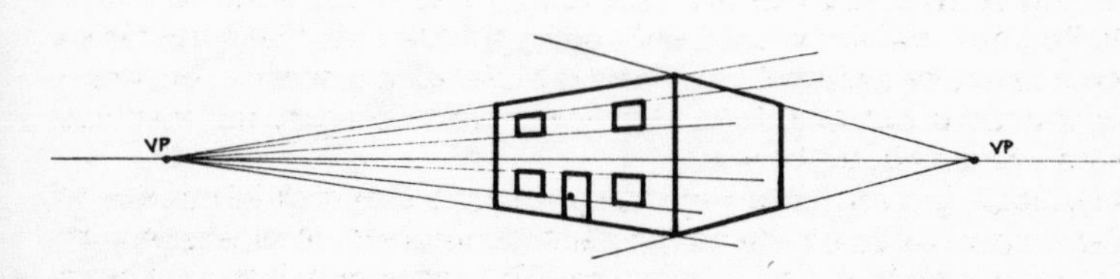

Figure 4

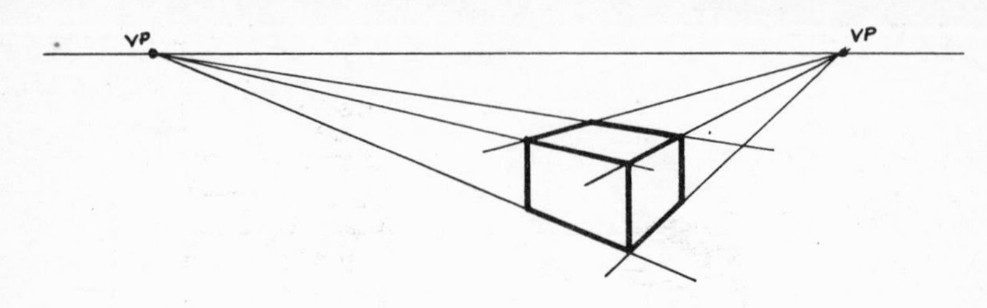

Figure 5

Let us represent the horizon by a straight line and focus attention upon just one point. We'll call this the 'vanishing point'. If we then radiate a few straight lines from this point they will begin to depict a sense of perspective. (See Figure 2.)

If we imagine ourselves on a road leading to the vanishing point, the road appears to become narrower and narrower until finally it is possible to observe it disappearing into the vanishing point. That is precisely why such points are known as vanishing points (Figure 3).

This principle can be applied to all three-dimensional objects in order to give them height, width and depth. To achieve this the horizon will need to be provided with two vanishing points Figure 4).

Your focal object need not be placed on the horizon, it can just as easily be above or below it. Simply follow the same principle of radiating lines from two vanishing points (Figure 5).

Foreground objects can be so close as to render their vanishing points too far apart for them to appear on the page (Figure 6).

When applying these principles of perspective you don't need to draw the vanishing points and guidelines radiating from them. You simply have to imagine them. This will help to give depth to your drawings no matter how simple they are.

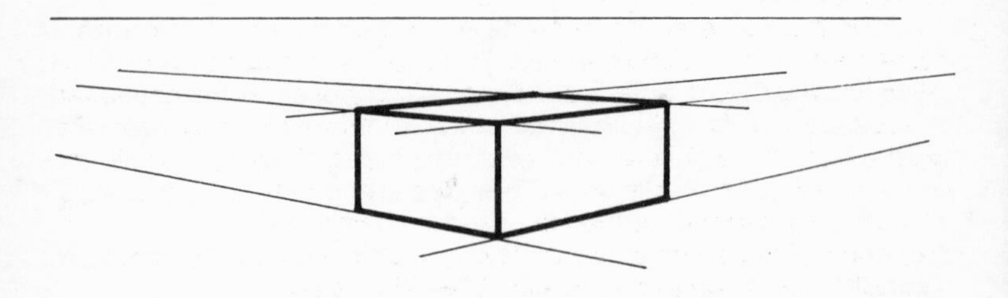

Figure 6

Try playing 'Over the Hills and Far Away' – then we may get some peace around here.
Figure 7

Perspective can aid scene-setting too, but it shouldn't be over-used. Backgrounds and incidental objects should be simple and light to avoid distracting the eye from the central theme of the drawing. This will usually be the characters of the piece who are likely to be positioned in the centre of the drawing. (See Figure 7.)

In this cartoon, just one everyday object, the armchair, is sufficient to establish a room setting. Often, one object is enough to set the scene; a punch bag will suggest a gymnasium; a beer glass a pub or bar; a tree an outdoor setting, and so on.

Cartoons can be either captioned or uncaptioned. In the uncaptioned cartoon the picture speaks for itself. Its success or otherwise relies heavily on the artistic ability of its composer. In the captioned cartoon the words will either complete the humour by supplementing the picture (neither words nor picture being able to stand alone), or the words of the joke would be understood without the picture. All but the gifted will opt for the captioned version.

A cartoon of mine published in *Review* didn't even hold perspective – simply two characters in profile. (See Figure 8.)

Before embarking on the final layout of your cartoon, make a rough draft to ensure correct proportions. This should be simple

'Have you been on that diet for long?'
Figure 8

enough to ensure it will register at a glance. Use a soft pencil for the outline, rubbing out and revising where necessary until you have the right balance. Your guidelines can be erased after inking in.

Keep finished lines bold and simple so they don't lose definition when reproduced. Editors like simple drawings. They are easier to reduce to fit limited space. Highly detailed drawings can have limited reduction potential.

As your artwork is likely to be reduced, its original size is relatively unimportant. I suggest an A5 sheet, filled. is the largest you should attempt in order to avoid the risk of definition loss during reduction. Leave a good margin all round, and write the caption well away from the body of the drawing; captions are often deleted from the artwork to be replaced by a typeset version.

Now all you have to think about is ideas.

Comic situations can be concocted from many everyday occurrences and human emotional responses: surprise, ridicule, inequality of status, banana skin situations, contrast, double meanings.

The jokes you hear at work could be developed into cartoon situations. Every time you hear laughter, make a note of what inspired it.

Study the cartoons in your everyday reading. Cut them out and file them under different situations and styles to assist with your future efforts. Alternative captions can often spring to mind when sifting through them.

The potential market for cartoons is vast. Just about any newspaper and magazine you pick up has one printed somewhere between its pages. Payment, of course, varies with the market, but the *Weekly News* pays around £5 per drawing whereas the *Daily Mirror* pays £25.

Puzzles and Posers

Miscellaneous Teasers

Take a look at any news-stand to see how many puzzle magazines are around today. There are dozens of them: *Popular Puzzles and Prizes, Word Finder, Codelink, Puzzler, Winner*, and many, many more.

At one time the majority of puzzle magazines were made up of crossword puzzles. These days puzzle formats are many and varied: spot the difference; photographs taken at odd angles; find the hidden words in a grid of letters; general knowledge quizzes; words forming diamonds, circles, spirals, figures of eight. Pick up any puzzle magazine and you will find scores of them. But of the variants to be found the majority use words in some form or another.

As puzzle types are so diverse it is difficult to be specific concerning rules of compilation. However, a study of how crosswords go together will be of benefit to those concerned with puzzles in general, as certain 'rules' have been established with precedent over the years. We'll deal with these in the next section.

Needless to say, some knowledge of English is required for such exercises, particularly in the case of spelling. A little inventiveness is also required, but the basic rules governing most puzzles will be relatively simple to pick up. Select two or three which particularly appeal to you and specialize in them; you will find they become easier to construct as you gain experience.

Those new to puzzle compilation might like to begin by looking at the *Mail on Sunday*. Their puzzle feature 'Dingbats' has become so popular that a board game based upon it is now available. Dingbats are puzzles, sent in by readers, which depict an arrangement of letters and symbols hiding a well-known phrase, name, or saying. £5 is paid for every one used. To give you an idea, here is one I've compiled:

UN   X

The solution here, in case you didn't get it, is: A French Kiss.

Crossword Puzzles

Pick up any newspaper and you are likely to find a crossword puzzle in its pages. Sometimes you'll find more than one: a cryptic version, a quick version, occasionally a children's version too.

Many magazines also carry crosswords. Potential markets are everywhere.

The level of difficulty of these puzzles varies greatly for both 'straight' and cryptic versions depending on the market. Some specialize in those for the novice, some for the enthusiast. Some use long words, some short words. Some require a dictionary to solve, others don't.

Whatever type and level of puzzle the compiler has in mind, the first thing to consider is the construction of the diagram. A study of the target publication will reveal what grid size to go for. A 15 X 15 grid is common.

Once you have chosen your grid, fill in all the black boxes (known as 'outs') to form a symmetrical pattern. Black boxes should be kept to a minimum if you are to be fair on your solver. The grid should allow enough intersections to be able to cross-check intersecting words. The aim should be to have equal numbers of checked and unchecked letters.

Those new to compilation should study diagrams used in target publications to get a feel for construction. Alternatively, copy one from a back issue – grids are not copyright. Crosswords only become copyright once they have taken form with the addition of clues.

Once your pattern is complete, number each box containing the first letter of both horizontal and vertical words. Your diagram is now finalized and ready to take solutions. Don't worry about clues at this stage, these will be invented *after* you are have found words to fit the grid.

The compilation of solutions is a matter of experimenting with different words until you have them to fit. Initially, this will be relatively easy but, without some knowledge of the tricks of the trade, there will come a time when those empty squares will stubbornly refuse to be filled. The way to avoid this situation is to endeavour to use those letters of the alphabet which are in most common use. These are:

E, T, A, O, I, N, S, H, R, D, L, U.

Try to avoid those letters least used, especially in the middle of words. The least used letters are:

X, Z, Q, V, G, K.

Where at all possible begin words with the seven most commonly used letters:

E, T, A, O, I, N, S.

Words containing vowels and consonants alternately are relatively easy to handle, whereas those containing consecutive vowels and consonants are not. Words like 'thriller' and 'pharmacy' are particularly difficult to contend with: each contains six consonants and just two vowels.

There will, of course, be times when you will be stuck for a one-word solution because you have run out of sensible letter options. When this happens you could consider splitting the solution to form two or, perhaps, more words. When this option also fails, there will be no alternative but to backtrack over what you have done, rearranging words in the grid local to your problem line until things finally fall into place.

An invaluable aid throughout all of this will be your dictionary, and more importantly your crossword dictionary. The layout of the latter is an invaluable aid to the compiler. Words are gathered together alphabetically according to the number of letters, beginning with just two, rising to eight, ten or sometimes more.

The next hurdle is the compilation of clues. With straight clues a simple word substitution is usually all that is needed. Look up your dictionary, or, more probably, your thesaurus of synonyms and antonyms, until you find a word best suited to the degree of difficulty of your chosen market.

Compiling cryptic clues demands a little more care as a number of principles have been established over the years, and yours should follow suit. Clues must be fair if the solver is not to feel cheated.

Possibly one of the most well known of clue types is the anagram. An anagram is the rearrangement of letters in a word or words so as to make another word or words. Clues need to contain some hint that the order of letters has changed by the use of such words as 'mixed', 'bent', or 'disturbed'. For example:

Clue:	Struck by a peculiar type of gloves (7).
Solution:	SMITTEN.
Reasoning:	The clue word here is STRUCK. The solution is an anagram of MITTENS which are a type of gloves. PECULIAR is the clue to the fact that a word has been mixed up.

The use of words within words is a common device. For example:

Clue:	Overthrown, feat indeed! (8)
Solution	DEFEATED.
Reasoning:	The clue word here is OVERTHROWN. The solution is in the word FEAT in DEED: DE-FEAT-ED.

Another form of words within words is the hidden word. This is very often a bit of a give away. The solution is literally found within the words of the clue. For example:

Clue: Old, found in stage dress. (4)
Solution: AGED.
Reasoning: The clue word here is OLD. The solution is found in ST(AGE D)RESS.

Word contraction is a well-used device. This is where part of a word in the clue provides the solution. For example:

Clue: Cut down on taxes. (3)
Solution: AXE.
Reasoning: The solution is to be found by the equivalent of the word CUT. If we cut T(AXE)S we find it.

A clue written in reverse order is commonly known as a reversal. When this device is used for a clue across, key words such as 'back' or 'retreats' are usually employed. When used for a down clue, words like 'up' or 'climbs' are applied. For example:

Clue: Step backwards for loved ones. (4)
Solution: PETS.
Reasoning: The clue words here are LOVED ONES. STEP backwards gives PETS.

Words are commonly represented by just a couple of letters. Doctor, for example, is known by the letters Dr; Bachelor of Arts by the letters BA; teetotaller by the letters TT. Abbreviations are often used to provide crossword solutions. For example:

Clue: Cross the motorway to mingle. (3)
Solution: MIX.
Reasoning: The clue word here is MINGLE. Cross is represented by the letter X, and motorway by M1.

Points of the compass are the most commonly used abbreviations. These are often referred to as 'a way' or 'a point', and are represented by the letters N, S, E, W. For example:

Clue: Quit over a point of silence. (5)
Solution: QUIET.
Reasoning: The clue word here is SILENCE. The point (of the compass) in this instance is E (east). Quit over E gives QUI(E)T.

Not all clues conveniently fall into any one category, but are often a mixture. For instance, a contraction could be added to an anagram. For example:

Clue:	Against some opponent getting a wrong dose. (7)
Solution:	OPPOSED.
Reasoning:	The clue word here is AGAINST. The solution is given by some OPPONENT = OPP getting a wrong DOSE = OSED. This produced OPP + OSED.

A similar derivation is when part of a word is added to another to form the solution. For example:

Clue:	Crack crevet in half in the end vice. (7)
Solution:	CREVICE.
Reasoning:	If we read the clue literally the solution will emerge automatically. Here the equivalent of CRACK is sought. CREVET in half gives CRE. In the end (of the solution) is VICE. This produces CRE-VICE.

Many hybrid clues are to be found in cryptic puzzles, limited only by the ingenuity of the compiler. New types of clue also emerge from time to time. All are legitimate providing they are seen to be fair-minded towards the solver. If you make up new rules ensure you stick to them throughout.

Another point to bear in mind when compiling clues is their bias. Many magazines, particularly specialist interest magazines, contain crosswords whose clues revolve around a particular theme. The writers' magazine *Freelance Writing and Photography*, for example, bought a puzzle of mine where all the clues revolved around the subject of freelance writing. The principle could just as easily be applied to any other subject: knitting, cooking, motoring, DIY, rope-making . . . anything. It is unlikely you would be 100 per cent successful in producing all clues relevant to a set theme, but those that aren't should not be totally alien. Here, try to provide solutions that would fit in with most themes.

Market study is as important for crossword puzzles as it is with any area of freelance writing. Ensure your offerings fit all aspects of the market: grid size, clue types, degree of difficulty.

Aim at the small magazines first. Don't worry too much if they don't currently carry crosswords; it is possible they don't simply because no one has offered them a regular supply. How many give-away papers in your area carry crossword puzzles? All of them? If not, try those that don't.

Click, Click

Snapshots

Most people own or have access to a camera these days. Often this is nothing more than a cartridge instamatic, but it suits most needs for holiday snaps, christenings, weddings, and the like. Sometimes, out of the hoards of headless portraits and fuzzy landscapes, there emerge some halfway decent photographs. It is these 'flukes' that you should examine to see if they could earn a pound or two from your favourite weekly's photo spot.

I doubt if many readers actually venture out specifically to take photographs for these features. Nearly always they prove suitable by chance. An apt picture emerges from the folder that comes back from the film processing laboratory with your holiday snaps in it. 'That's just right for *Bella*', you say. Off it goes in the hope of a handsome cheque; let's face it, over 100 are used in this magazine every year, so yours has to have a chance.

But you could improve your chances even more if you decided to approach these features in a more methodical manner. Whenever you go out be on the lookout for anything unusual that could make an interesting feature. Have your camera with you whenever possible. You never know when you're likely to see a traffic warden getting a ticket, or a man biting a dog.

Research those magazines using reader features to examine how others have done it. Ask yourself: how could I produce a new slant on what's been used? Then get your camera out and have a go. Film is cheap these days so keep clicking away.

The satirical magazine *Private Eye* use an amusing photograph in each issue under their headline 'I-Spy'. Very often this depicts an unusual sign. One they used was of a cleaner's shop in New York whose address was 10 Downing Street. This earned the photographer £10.

What are your local shops called? Are there any you could use? There is a butcher's shop near to me that I wouldn't mind a steak in; it is called T. Bone. Very apt. A photograph of their sign underlined by a witty caption would make an interesting filler.

Bella invites you to send in your favourite snaps. They publish two every week. 'They can be funny or they can be cute or they can be your own undiscovered works of art. Only your own pictures, though. Let us know where and when you took them and give us your name and address and telephone number. We will pay £50 if we publish your picture!' One issue carried these two items: A little girl apparently kissing a puppy on the mouth: the caption read 'Puppy Love'. The other photo depicted a kitten standing on its hind legs with a ball of wool in its paws. The caption read 'Well held, sir!'

Do you have pets that get themselves into interesting or humorous situations?

The glossy magazine *Best* uses a photograph in their 'Double Take' feature every week. They say: 'If you have an amusing, strange or wacky photograph at home, why not send it in to us?' One issue pictured a young girl with a horse. The girl was clearly enjoying the attentions of the horse which was affectionately nuzzling her chest. This picture earned a fiver.

Do your children have a natural attraction for animals?

Amateur Photographer publish a reader's photograph every week in their 'Top Shot' feature. This forms part of their letters page which pays £10. One they printed showed a pedestrian suspension bridge among several trees.

Are there any scenes of natural beauty near you that could make this slot?

All of these features provide a suitable outlet for the happy 'snap-taker' with an eye for the unusual. But for the more ambitious David Baileys among you, a slightly more up-market approach is the order of the day.

Photography

As we have seen, it is possible to take saleable photographs with some simple equipment and very little knowledge of photographic techniques. Usually, one of the cartridge camera types designed for the novice is good enough for readers' features too. Beyond that they are not generally suited to freelance work.

Of the better equipment available, the 35 mm camera is the most widely used by amateur and professional photographers alike. It is ideally suited to freelance work and is readily available in many high street photographic shops.

The standard of 35 mm equipment varies greatly, as does the cost. By and large you get what you pay for, and the more sophisticated the equipment, the more it will cost. Let us examine the basics.

There are two ways in which camera equipment can view its subject. The simplest of these is the viewfinder camera. This type has two lenses. In addition to the lens which transfers the image to the film, a viewfinder lens is provided to focus on the subject. Because these lenses are separate mechanisms the picture presented to the film is not exactly the same as that presented to the eye through the viewfinder. This set-up is usually accurate enough for medium-to-long shots, but the closer you get to the subject the greater the chances the image will become cropped in the final picture.

The single lens reflex (SLR) camera houses a device to allow the subject to be viewed directly through the picture-taking lens. In other words, what you see through the viewfinder will end up on film.

Not all viewfinder cameras will allow an interchange of lenses, whereas most SLR cameras will. SLR cameras are more expensive than viewfinder cameras but for the more serious freelance endeavouring to sell his work they can be a worthwhile investment. Both types of camera are available in either manual or automatic versions.

In the manual camera the operator has to set the exposure controls; the automatic camera does this itself. Two variables determine exposure: the shutter speed and the aperture size. The shutter speed determines how long the film is to be exposed to the light of the image passing through the lens. The aperture sets the size of the opening through which the light passes.

Automatic cameras work by adjusting either the shutter speed or the aperture size, or by a combination of both. In the latter the camera controls 'read' the total amount of light received from the aperture and shutter settings to determine exposure.

The advantage to the beginner of the automatic over the manual camera will be all too obvious. The only worry is focusing – and even this can be eliminated on some cameras.

While focusing traditionally is done manually, these days the autofocus lens is becoming widely used. The lens is focused by a motor which is automatically activated by either an infra-red beam or an image contrast technique. These are truly fully automatic cameras where all the operator has to do is press the button. Needless to say, they are expensive.

Focus determines sharpness. An in-focus photograph will have well-defined lines; an out-of-focus one will be blurred.

In the majority of cartridge cameras the lens is pre-focused at a set distance. This can be achieved because the lenses used have a very short focal length which provides a great depth of field. This enables the subject to stay in focus over a large range of distances.

With simple viewfinder cameras focusing is done by setting the estimated distance of the subject on the focusing mount on the lens. The mount will be graded either in symbols or on a scale in feet or metres. An alternative method is the rangefinder. Focusing by this system is done while looking through the viewfinder. An optical device creates two images which must be merged to form one when the mount is rotated to the correct distance.

Whatever the method used, it is the lens that finally transfers the image to the film. The fundamental difference between lenses is their focal length. This determines how much of a scene will be included in the picture. A 20 mm wide-angle lens, for example, will capture a panoramic view, whereas an 800 mm telephoto lens will cover a smaller area far into the distance. In other words, the greater the focal length the more it will magnify.

Your choice of film will depend upon a number of factors, not the least of which will be your chosen market. Some editors use only black and white photographs; others prefer colour. Either way, if you find yourself in a corner, colour prints can be made from your slides and slides can be made from negative film.

By far the greatest editorial demand is for black and white prints, followed by colour transparencies. There is little demand for colour prints.

Black and white pictures should be printed on glossy paper only of 125 mm × 175 mm or preferably 200 mm × 250 mm. For colour work, 35 mm transparencies are often acceptable, but in some cases, particularly for cover shots, they should be at least 60 mm × 60 mm.

Film for colour transparencies can be obtained for use in natural or artificial light so it is important to see you have the right one.

Film speed should be selected according to prevailing lighting conditions and the speed of action, if any, to be photographed.

The most common measure of film speed is its ASA rating. These are as designated by the American Standards Association and are printed on film boxes. Ratings range from 25 to 1000 ASA; the higher the number the more sensitive is the film to light. For static daylight conditions the most common choice of film is 100 ASA. For poorer lighting conditions, where no flash is to be used, a higher rating is needed. Fast films are useful when covering action shots. They require less light to expose them so faster shutter speeds can be used to help prevent blurred images.

Once you have all the mechanics sorted out, and have selected your camera, you'll need to consider how you'll use it. Earlier, we discussed depth of field. Now we'll consider this further for the sake of technique.

Depth of field is that zone in front and behind the plane of sharpest focus in which the image remains acceptably sharp. Beyond this zone the images lose definition and become blurred. The greater the depth of field, the greater this zone of sharpness becomes. As a general principle, the closer you are to your subject, the smaller will be the depth of field.

Another factor to be considered is aperture. In addition to determining exposure, aperture also changes the depth of field; the smaller the aperture the greater the depth of field. And remember, the greater the 'F' number the smaller the aperture. Put simply:

For a small depth of field use a low 'F' number.

For a large depth of field use a high 'F number.

Once you have gained confidence, it is a good idea to try a number of shots at different aperture settings.

The exposure setting determines how much light the film is to receive. When the film receives the correct amount of light, the resultant photograph is balanced in its shades of light and dark. When the film receives too much light (overexposed) the picture will be pale and washed out. If it doesn't receive enough light (underexposed) the picture will be too dark. Experiment with exposure. Try one setting above and one setting below the proper exposure. Take plenty of shots; film is cheap.

It is important to ensure your photographs are sharply in focus with good contrast. Pictures composed entirely of shades of grey have little impact. The same principle can be applied to colour transparencies; solid, rich colours are needed if they are to grab attention.

When it comes to composition, knowing what you want to show in the frame is the major part of the battle. All too often the subject is too far away. As a general principle, get in close. The objective of your composition is to centre the viewer's attention on the subject. So fill the frame with it.

Keep compositions simple. No heavy superfluous background images. No telegraph poles 'growing' out of your subject's head. No shadows blocking out half the action.

People become very self-conscious when they know they are being photographed, so try to take your shot when they least expect it. Or better still, try to capture them when they are unaware of your presence.

Once you have come to terms with your camera, both with the mechanics and with the techniques, you will have to think about markets. The same principles of market research that apply to writing apply equally to photographs. See what is being used by various publications and offer them more of the same.

Have another look at the readers' spots first. You are bound to stand a better chance with your new equipment. And some readers' features earn £50 per time. Not bad at all. But then, money isn't everything. Not to begin with anyway.

Another good beginners' market is local newspapers – and in particular the free sheets. Be careful though, not all will offer a fee. So if money is important to you, check first – but remember some experience is better than none.

There are so many give-away papers nowadays, and they generally have so few staff, that they are often crying out for halfway decent pictures.

I once took my camera to a charity fund-raising children's tea party and shot a roll of film. Unfortunately, not having my own processing equipment, I had no way of getting the film processed quickly. So I rang one of the local free sheets. They developed and printed the film for me, printed a lovely picture of my daughter in the next issue, and gave me two rolls of film into the bargain. And it was all good experience.

Those scribes writing articles can often give their submissions more of a chance of being accepted by submitting them with a photograph or two. An eye-catching picture can set your article above the field even before it has been read. If magazines usually carry illustrations it stands to reason that it will be much easier for the editor if he doesn't have to find his own.

Happy clicking.

Articles

Expanding Your Horizons

Once you have gained some experience with shorter freelance work you may wish to consider expanding your horizons. But to write longer pieces you need to enjoy the writing process itself. While many people are in their element rummaging through books and papers unearthing facts for their fillers, they sometimes find the more expansive creative writing process a difficult task, for longer pieces require more input than just the facts. They take creativity and concerted effort. But you will never know whether this is for you until you try.

Essentially, articles are comprised of a subject, relevant facts (plus sometimes some anecdotal material), a set number of words, and an individual style.

Subject

Before you can begin writing your article you have to know roughly what it is to be about. What material is suitable for an article? Well, almost anything if it is written up in an interesting enough way.

As a general principle, writing about anything of which you have a first-hand knowledge will come easier than a subject you would have to research. Articles written around personal experience usually sound as though the writer knows the subject. Editors like authoritative pieces, so the more you know of your subject the better.

Begin with what you know best: your job, your hobby, your last holiday, that recent business trip. Analyse everything.

Someone in the plumbing trade, for instance, could write an article (or, indeed a series of articles) on how the DIY enthusiast could install a central heating boiler. A bricklayer could describe how to build a garden wall or how to knock down a chimney breast. A keen gardener could advise on how to cultivate prize-winning marrows.

But be honest about the selection of your subject-matter. Knowledge alone is not enough; it must also be interesting. No matter how much you enjoyed making sandcastles with your children on the beach, potential readers are hardly likely to share your enthusiasm. Unless, of course, there is something special about your sandcastles. While on holiday in Cyprus a few years ago I watched spellbound as a hippy-looking chap produced a beautiful sculptured bust from a pile of wet sand. By the time he had completed his masterpiece a crowd had gathered and cameras were clicking wildly. This incident was different enough to be of interest to potential article readers. A photograph together with a write-up covering the relevant who, what, why, when, where and how, would have made a sale, I'm sure.

'Write about what you know' is a well-worn maxim in writing circles, but one we'll take one final look at. Some years ago I submitted a couple of manuscripts to a magazine specializing in the theme of small business. The subject of my articles was only loosely related to the theme of the magazine but none the less I felt it would interest its readers. The first piece was accepted without comment, but the second acceptance was accompanied by a letter from the editor. He liked my writing style and asked if I would be prepared to become a regular contributor to his magazine. Would I! Frankly, I knew little of the subject of small business – but I soon began to learn. Eventually I became knowledgeable enough to produce twelve articles a year without difficulty. So, with the experience in mind, I can comfortably advise others to modify the maxim to 'Write about what you can comfortably get to know.'

Having said that, don't write on any subject it would normally take a specialist to cover. Medical matters, for example, should be left to those properly qualified to deal with them.

Whenever you read something – your daily or local newspaper, book, catalogue, whatever – be on the lookout for interesting facts and ideas. Then make a written note of them in your ideas book. Selling subjects are: money, love, personal popularity, leisure, self-improvement, DIY, entertainment.

Ensure your research is thorough and accurate. Use several sources as a cross-check. It is always better to have too much material than too little. You can always discard what you cannot use. Or better still, you may have enough left over for another article. (There's more about fact-finding in Chapter 3.)

Making Use of Your Facts

Once you have the basic idea for your article sit down and make some notes. Jot down anything entering your head, no matter how random. Leave a space beneath each topic as you go. This way, when you have exhausted your ideas, you can separate them by tearing them into strips. These can then be sorted and laid out in a coherent order. They can then be stuck or stapled to sheets of paper to form your final notes. I have heard that some authors use index cards for this process, each bearing a single topic. Use whatever routine works best for you.

Before you sort your facts, formulate your basic structure. An article should be made up of a beginning, a middle and an end. The beginning must hook your readers' attention in some way, the middle should present the facts or the arguments, the ending should succinctly summarize the theme. With this in mind, sort your thoughts into order.

Writing the first paragraph is usually the biggest hurdle. An opening can take as much effort as the remainder of the piece. Your first paragraph should be handled in such a way that it motivates the readers to read on. If it doesn't, they may give up after the first few sentences.

There are numerous tricks to overcome this problem. One of the following as, or as part of, your opening sentence is usually all you will need:

- A question
- A statement
- A quotation
- An anecdote
- A fact
- A statistic

Here are a couple of examples.

One of my articles appearing in *Business Head Start* began:

> A very profitable business emerging now in the trade is original oil paintings.

Here a statement is used to get straight to the theme of the piece.

Another of my articles, appearing in *Freelance Writing and Photography*, began:

> Do the characters in your short stories have too much to say for themselves?

This question was designed to identify with fiction writers to encourage them to read on.

Get the idea?

Whichever of these opening gambits you choose, you should ensure it is relevant to the main body of your article; not just a 'trick' to hook your reader. Otherwise you'll lose credibility.

Once you have your readers' interest you must maintain it right to the end. Lay out your facts in an interesting and coherent manner. Answer questions in the readers' mind. In long passages, use anecdotes to liven interest. A book of quotations is useful here.

And when you get to the end of your piece, don't stop dead. This will leave your reader feeling dissatisfied. Your ending should sum up the points you have made in snappy fashion.

Throughout all of this you will have to bear length in mind. Can your subject sustain the facts for a long article? Or is the subject too broad for the brief outline you have in mind? Some themes are only good for a mere 500 words or so, whereas others are deep enough for several thousand.

More importantly, what is the average length of articles used by your target market? Look to see what the average length of articles used by your selection publication is. If this is 1000 words, stick to it rigidly; no matter how well written a 3000-word piece happens to be, it will not be published.

Style

An article composed of little but facts is unlikely to sustain interest. Your words must entertain. Use colourful expression coupled with anecdotal material, bearing in mind your target market.

Use current language. I was raised in the days of Imperial measurements, good old feet and inches. Mention this to current primary school children and they will have little, if any, comprehension of what you are talking about.

Avoid ambiguity. If something is big, be specific – say how big. The word big is a relative term. A bird is big in comparison with a worm, but it is small in comparison with a dog. The term 'handful' conveys more than the term 'few'. 'Over the horizon' imparts more to the reader than 'a long way'.

Beginning writers often have a leaning to flowery language. This is usually a mistake. Simple words and simple sentences make easy reading. But you must bear in mind your proposed publication all the same. Does it use short sentences or long sentences? Or something in between?

You can sometimes make your writing snappier by splitting a sentence into two. If a sentence rambles on you are probably trying to say too much at once anyway.

Examine paragraph length too. A paragraph may be a single sentence or several sentences. Vary paragraph lengths. This will add variety of pace and create visual interest.

Don't worry too much about grammar. As a general principle if your writing is easy to read, people will read it. But again, even simple writing has to conform to the style of your market. You will no doubt be anxious to develop your own style, but this must always be in keeping with editorial requirements.

The title of your article is the first thing your intended editor will see. So it must grab attention. Try to find a title that fits, that says something of the theme of your piece.

Occasionally an editor will change a title. This has happened only a couple of times to me, but it has happened none the less. If it happens to you, ask yourself why. Does the editor's choice more succinctly summarize the theme? Or is it perhaps just shorter than yours?

A phrase from the body of the article can often make an attention-grabbing title. One of my articles, on the subject of mail order selling, was entitled 'The Right Response'. This phrase was also used as the last three words of the article.

A play on words can provide a good headline. These have worked for me: 'The Write Course?' headed an article about freelance writing correspondence courses. 'There's Money in Oil' described how to import original oil paintings from Hong Kong.

No matter how you slant your title, ensure it is short. Editors are plagued with space restrictions, so try to avoid anything over five or six words.

Markets

The logical starting point for the beginner trying to find article markets are those periodicals inviting readers' submissions. Mostly, these are autobiographical pieces which means research is easy, the subject is easy, and in all probability the writing will be easy too.

A good starting point is the *Weekly News* – they'll even help you with the writing. They say:

> If you've had to face up to a big problem in life, your story could give courage to others in similar circumstances. Send a letter to 'My Problem', giving brief details. We'll help with the writing. The same goes for the story of your unusual romance. Details, please, to 'Love Story'. A £25 award is paid for every one printed.

One of the submissions I read contained 1100 words, which seems to be typical of the length generally used.

The baby magazine *Young Mother* carries a reader's article in each issue. They ask:

> Have you ever wanted to get on a 'Soapbox' and let off steam about some topic that you really feel strongly about? Well here's your chance to do it in each issue of *Young Mother*. Write your views (in not more than 750 words, please) and send to Soapbox, Young Mother, Owen Road, Diss, Norfolk, IP22 3HH; the sender of the one to be published will receive a book token for £10.

A slightly better paying market is the young family magazine *Under Five*. Their invitation says:

> Do you feel strongly about something? Write and tell us about it in 750 words – we'll pay you £30 if we publish it. Write to us at Soapbox, Under Five, 71 Newcomen Street, London, SE1 1YT.

Once you have conquered the readers' submissions market you can think of expanding your horizons. Don't forget to continue to target your article before you write it. Don't write to suit yourself then try to find a market for it. The chances are it will boomerang back time and again. Write for a specific magazine using a compatible style.

Begin your speculative offerings with small circulation magazines. Contact your local give-away papers to see what scope there is for the freelancer. In my area alone, four free papers fall through our letterbox each week. These often carry freelance material.

You should also consider one of the many small press magazines in circulation. More of this later.

Short Stories

The Long and The Short of it

The word 'short' is a relative term. Short stories can vary in length from just a few hundred to several thousand words: it all depends on the market. But no matter how limited the allocation of words, each short story will have a beginning, a middle and an end. The treatment of these elements can vary greatly from one story to another, but each has an important part to play.

In common with most written forms, the opening of a short story is a key element. The first few sentences must arrest the readers' attention in some way if it is to entice them to read on. One method of doing this is to give your readers a hint of the problem your theme character is to encounter later on.

Introduce your theme character at the earliest opportunity; often the reader will identify with the first person encountered.

Once you have your readers' attention the middle of the story can unfold. This presents the problems to be faced by the theme character and shows how he reacts to them. Each time he deals with one problem he is presented with a greater one.

The end of the story contains the climax. This reveals how the theme character faces up to, and overcomes, the biggest hurdle. The conclusion should be as brief as possible so it leaves your reader satisfied but wanting more. Too much said after the major conflict has been resolved tends to dilute the climax.

Woven through the three preceding parts of a short story are five other elements. These are:

1 The plot
2 The theme
3 The setting
4 Characterization
5 Style

The Plot

To many fiction writers, plotting can be the most difficult of their writing tasks, the part requiring that sparkle of originality which all too often eludes them. But this should not be the case.

Established story writers have long accepted that there are no new plots, only a small number of basic situations around which all fiction revolves. One exponent of this theory was Gozzi, who maintained that there are only thirty-six dramatic situations upon which all drama is founded. When first confronted by this idea, many would-be authors baulk at it as absurd. But in his book *The Thirty-Six Dramatic Situations*, George Polti sets out to demonstrate the Gozzi theory and does so very convincingly. His book lays down each situation in turn, together with a description and literary examples of each. I am not suggesting the beginning writer should necessarily read this book (you may find it a little dry anyway), simply to accept the idea behind it. With this in mind, writers should never have to use the excuse that they are stuck for an idea. But more of this in a minute.

Once a theme situation has been established, the author has to decide how to turn the idea into an entire plot.

Fundamentally, plots are about conflict and how the theme character reacts to that conflict. In most popular fiction the hero overcomes all of his problems to produce a satisfactory conclusion – the classic happy ending. Stories which end with the theme character failing to attain his goal are, of course, published, but they are usually skilfully written by masters of the genre. It is far easier to win a reader's affection with stories that conclude sympathetically, and so it is advisable to twist all plots to suit this approach.

If we accept this proposal we can reduce all plots to four basic elements:

1 The central character has an objective.
2 The central character is presented with obstacles and complications which make it difficult to achieve this objective.
3 The obstacles and complications increase in intensity until they look as though they will overwhelm the central character and frustrate all attempts to attain the goal.
4 The central character overcomes the problems to produce a satisfactory conclusion.

In choosing a storyline for your plot, it is important to avoid outrageous situations. Your plots must be contained within the bounds of reason if your reader is to believe in them. Don't have your athlete run a mile in 1½ minutes – it just isn't possible.

Having said that, a large number of short stories published in the popular press are pure escapism. Not all will be in this category, but a great number are. Readers will readily identify with the ticket clerk who becomes a airline pilot, or the make-up artist who becomes a leading actress. People like to dream, so encourage them – but make it believable.

If you have little or no knowledge of the facts surrounding your story you must undertake some research. It is not enough to say the nephew poisoned his rich aunt in order to inherit her wealth. That would be too shallow. You must say what the poison was and, perhaps, what were its effects – different poisons cause different symptoms. Copper sulphate introduced into the diet, for example, must be used over a long period of time. Its effects are: at first indigestion, followed by wasting (giving the appearance of chronic infections of the intestines), then ultimately death. The effects of strychnine, on the other hand, are relatively quick and quite violent: fits, followed by suffocation or death by exhaustion.

Make your research thorough.

All stories, whether escapist or otherwise, are about conflict and how the theme character responds to that conflict. And bear in mind your theme character must have a strong motivation to solve the problem of his conflict. If he hasn't, you have no story.

Endeavour to make your reader care what happens to your newly introduced central character; to sympathize with him over the complications which threaten to frustrate his objective.

Among the negative influences in your story, try to introduce one which endeavours, intentionally or otherwise, to steer your theme character onto the wrong path. It must not succeed, of course, but it must be presented in such a way that it will seem logical to the reader.

Put strong pressure on your central character to take negative action. If he is being pursued by the police, however innocent he may be, introduce influences which make him want to give himself up, even though he knows his case will look pretty hopeless unless he can find the guilty party himself. This influence can come from many quarters: from his family, for him to do the 'right thing', or perhaps from the elements – he has become so cold and hungry the thought of being warm and fed will seem a very appealing alternative to being on the run.

In the *very* short story there will be insufficient time to deal with more than one complication, so stage two of the plotting process would be omitted. In the longer story there would be numerous second-stage conflicts that build in intensity until they reach the third stage complication: the climax.

When you get to the climax don't end your story unsympathetically. Stories where the heroine dies in the last paragraph do get published, but are always skilfully written. It is better you steer clear of any storyline which ends with the central character failing to achieve her objective.

It is important for the central character to solve the final problem herself – should an incidental character resolve her difficulties the reader will feel let down. But don't allow your central character to pull rabbits out of hats – if she needs a short length of wire to pick a lock in her time of crisis ensure your reader knows well in advance that she carries a piece in her pocket.

Having said all that, let us now have a go at constructing a complete plot. These days, a great deal of popular fiction revolves around romance, so let's construct a plot to suit a typical women's magazine using the four-point plan:

1 The central character falls in love with a girl and intends to marry her. (Objective.)
2 The girl's parents object to the marriage, for example, on the grounds that the central character is of a lower social class and is unfit to take the hand of their daughter. He is a penniless light aircraft pilot employed as a crop-sprayer. The parents, on the other hand, are from the landed gentry. Remember, though, to make your central character acceptable to your reader. Weatherworn he might be, but you should avoid making him a complete anti-hero. Your reader must like your central character if he is to care what happens to him. (Complications.)
3 The parents send their daughter to finishing school in Switzerland, thus severing the couple's association. (Escalating complications.)
4 The daughter is kidnapped for a ransom her parents cannot pay. The central character uses his piloting skills to rescue her from a remote hideout. The parents are eternally grateful to him and so allow the couple to marry. (Satisfactory conclusion.)

So there we have it, a complete story outline.

So What's the Big Idea?

The theme of the story is the recurrent subject upon which the plot is based; it is the important *idea* behind the story, or, if you like, the theme is the message.

For example, let us take a poor nineteenth-century country boy who has never had the benefit of a proper schooling, who has no shoes, and who often goes hungry. Despite his poor background he works hard until one day he has saved sufficient funds to attempt the journey to London, where, he has been led to believe, the streets are paved with gold. But alas, when he arrives in the city he finds the streets are dirty and poverty is all around. The theme of this story is clearly 'the grass is always greener in the other field'. It summarizes in one short sentence what the central character has learned from the events of the story.

Some of the more popular women's magazines stress the theme

very strongly, while the better quality end of the market simply *imply* the theme.

The theme should slowly unfold throughout the story as the central character tries to unravel his problem. And by the end of the final complication, the climax, the theme should be fully revealed.

As we said earlier, thinking up plots can sometimes prove difficult so any pointers to help in this direction will be welcome. Beginning with a well-known theme can often get the mind working. Listed below are a number of common sayings to help you:

- Crime does not pay.
- Spare the rod and spoil the child.
- Don't let your heart rule your head.
- Beauty is in the eye of the beholder.
- Life begins at forty.
- A stitch in time saves nine.
- A little is better than none.
- It is never too late.
- A miss is as good as a mile.
- Blood is thicker than water.
- Don't count your chickens before they are hatched.
- Too many cooks spoil the broth.
- Many hands make light work.
- Better late than never.
- A fool and his money are soon parted.
- Not all that glistens is gold.
- One man's meat is another man's poison.
- Beauty is only skin deep.
- Life is what you make it.
- Pride comes before a fall.
- Every dog has his day.
- Self-denial is good for the soul.
- The grass is always greener in the other field.
- What is good for the goose is good for the gander.
- There is no smoke without fire.
- Every cloud has a silver lining.
- Where there is a will there is a way.
- One good turn deserves another.

The Setting

Fiction can be set in:

- The present
- The past
- The future
- At home

- Abroad
- In imaginary worlds

How you describe the setting surrounding the events of your story will depend upon your writing style, the length of your story, where the events are to take place, whether or not your theme character is familiar with his surroundings.

A first-person narrative means the environment will be described exclusively in the thoughts and senses of the theme character. The third-person approach avoids such restrictions.

The balance between dialogue and narrative will also have a bearing on how the setting is to be revealed. In many a modern first-person tale, a large proportion of the setting is described by way of dialogue.

In the *short* short story the allocation of the number of words in itself can hold its own restrictions. Every word must go towards the telling of the tale – there aren't enough vividly to describe the setting.

Should your theme character land on a far distant planet you will need to describe the setting in some detail, otherwise your reader will be unable to gain a feel for the place. A London location, on the other hand, can take a brief mention of Big Ben to create the image of big city surroundings.

When your theme character is at home in his living room he won't constantly ponder the colour of the curtains; he will be too familiar with them to give them a second thought. Conversely, when he visits a foreign land for the first time he will take a detailed note of his surroundings.

Characterization

If your fictional characters are to be believable they must look and behave like real people. Believable characters make believable stories.

The most important character in your story is your protagonist. If your reader is to care what happens to her she must be able to identify with her. One way to achieve this is to research the readership of your target publication and create your theme character to suit. Mould your characters around a composite of these.

This approach won't be right for every situation, of course. Take a story surrounding a young boy which is targeted at a retirement magazine, for example. Here you would need to play on the sympathies of the reader as a grandparent, perhaps.

If you are to achieve reader identification for your main character you must make him likeable. The conquering hero of a war story could be brave and a natural leader whereas a heroine of a nature magazine would love wild life.

Don't make your characters superhuman (the exceptions here, perhaps, are spoofs and science fiction). Don't endow your central character with the strength of ten men – make him lose the odd skirmish. You will endear him to your reader more easily. And don't have the greengrocer pick up an opaque object from the beach and recognize it as a valuable uncut diamond; he simply wouldn't have the ability. Neither would a frail old lady have the strength to cudgel her fifteen stone nephew to death; she would need to select some gentler, more manageable approach, such as poisoning.

There is so much that can be said about a character there is a real danger of saying too much. The trick is to isolate a few salient features and express them vividly. If you repeat these characteristics early on in your story your reader will remember them.

The first thing is to name your characters. Choose names with different sounds. Norton is too like Norman to be used in the same story; it could confuse your reader.

What about the appearance of your character? Is he fat, thin, tall, short, muscular, weedy, young, old? Does he smile, frown, cough, laugh, spit? How much does he have to say for himself? Is he the silent type, or a non-stop chatterbox? Does he have a high voice, low voice, squeaky voice, a lisp, an accent? Is he fair-skinned, dark-skinned, wrinkled, scarred? Does he have red hair, black hair, curly hair, straight hair, or is he balding? Are his clothes the height of fashion or tatty and torn? How does he stand, walk, sit, run? What of his mannerisms? Does he scratch his head, pick his nose, cock an eyebrow, stoop, stagger?

Select the key features you wish to portray and characterize them.

Examine the people you know to identify their major characteristics. Composites of these are sure to be believable.

Another aid to behavioural characteristics is the study of astrological signs. The twelve signs of the zodiac provide an excellent source of character material. Here are their main features:

Capricorn: Ambitious. Often perfectionists. Stubborn at times. Outwardly modest, though inwardly they possess an iron determination.

Aquarius: Kind. Sympathetic. Often a little difficult to understand. They are inclined to the arts, music and literature. Studious and deep thinking. Intuitive. Independent. Self-willed.

Pisces: Kind. Sympathetic. Patient. Generous. Often indecisive. Can be depressed by trivial worries. Often dreamers. Animal lovers.

Aries: The strongest of all the astrological signs. Headstrong. Impulsive. Always want to be on top. They

	make rulers and pioneers. They like to give orders not take them. They like to travel.
Taurus:	Practical. Solid. Patient. Reliable. Honest. They make good doctors and bankers.
Gemini:	Intelligent. Critical. Analytical. Sometimes nomadic due to a love of change. Can be very determined. Quick-witted. Inclined to worry.
Cancer:	Generous. Sensitive. Romantic. Home-loving. They like to be noticed despite an unassuming façade. Can be very contrary. They love antiques and anything of age.
Leo:	Determined. Frank and open. Good listeners. Perfectionists. Self-confident. Prone to depression.
Virgo:	Intelligent. Methodical. Critical. Down-to-earth. They have a flair for business but are not front-runners.
Libra:	Refined. Artistic. Generous. Friendly. Perceptive. Fair-minded. Loyal to their friends.
Scorpio:	Discreet. Cautious. Crafty. Shrewd judge of people. Often jealous.
Sagittarius:	Happy. Optimistic. Energetic. Loyal. Demonstrative in relationships. Open. Frank. Untidy.

Style

Style is that quality in writing which sets one author's work apart from another. If you like, it is the author's literary signature. And because it is unique is it a difficult skill to teach. In the main, it must be acquired by patient practice.

Style is a question of approach, of how the essentials are assembled and presented in the telling of the story.

Remember, always *show* the reader what is happening; never *tell*. Here is an example of telling:

> Robert loved cats.

Here is an example of showing:

> Robert stopped to avoid the cat half-hidden in the shadows. He crouched to stroke its tabby fur. 'I'd move over if I were you,' he said. 'Someone may step on you.'

Choice of viewpoint is another important consideration. Are you going to have your theme character tell the reader of her experiences, or are you going to do it for her?

To many beginning writers the first-person viewpoint can be very tempting because, they believe, it will add immediacy to their writing. But this approach is by no means as simple to handle as it may appear.

First of all, the central character can only relate to what she can see and hear and so cannot describe other scenes that occur in parallel. Neither can she know what someone else is doing elsewhere since she cannot be there to observe what is happening.

As the first-person viewpoint is focused on just one character, only her thoughts can be used. You cannot let your reader into the mind of anyone else to learn what they are thinking.

Lastly, the reader knows the first-person character has survived the ordeal because she is alive to tell her story. And this can be a very important consideration if you want to keep your reader in suspense over the future well-being of your central character.

Many restrictions imposed by the first-person approach do not apply to the third-person story. In this the viewpoint can legitimately be switched from the protagonist to another character. Granted, this must be undertaken with care if your reader is not to become confused and lose sympathy with the protagonist's viewpoint, but it is legitimate none the less. As a general rule it is wise to keep the changed viewpoint as short as possible. And under no circumstances continually switch from one viewpoint to another.

In the more popular markets stories are often composed almost entirely of dialogue, whereas in some of the higher-quality markets a great deal of narrative is used. It is a question of market research. Study those magazines to which you wish to contribute to see what balance they use.

The length of a short story will also influence its style. The novel has sufficient scope to allow the characters to show themselves in depth. Some novels house two dozen personalities or more, all of whom are described in vivid detail. The short story, however, allows no such extravagance. Particularly the *short* short story of around 500–1000 words. These can describe three or four characters at most.

But no matter what length your short story, it will contain the same basic elements inherent in all stories. We shall reiterate an earlier statement by saying that stories are composed of a beginning, a middle and an end. The beginning will introduce your central character (if possible within the first paragraph) and will outline his problems; the middle will contain the escalating crises; the end will unveil the satisfactory conclusion. The pace with which these events take place will depend upon two factors. First, the number of words allotted to the task, and second, to the nature of the plot. Overall, the thriller will need to be composed predominantly of fast, dramatic actions, while the romance will need to be more leisurely. But whatever the subject-matter, all stories share one thing in common: the pace will pick up towards the climax.

When you have the first draft of your story you may find it to be too long or too short. If it is too short for your intended market you will need to expand it. Be careful to avoid padding though. In particular, avoid anything – narrative or dialogue – that does not further the storyline in some way. Make additional words count by using them to strengthen a character trait, give more feeling to a setting, heighten the emotional involvement of your reader.

Cutting a manuscript is usually easier than expanding it. Ask yourself: if I leave it out will it matter? Despite that you should always have in mind the maxim 'make every word count', you will usually find some way in which to cut unnecessary words. And if your story is much too long try to combine sentences and paragraphs. Quite often a manuscript will benefit from careful pruning by becoming more tightly written.

Markets

By far the biggest market for short stories is the popular women's magazines. An understanding publisher of these is D. C. Thompson. They always encourage emerging talent and will even comment upon a rejected script if it shows promise. Their approach is, unfortunately, rare these days.

D. C. Thompson's guidelines for their women's magazines tell you what they are looking for:

> Romantic or dramatic stories where the human or love interest is strong. Stories reflecting the romance, the adventure, the emotional drama which arise in everyday life to the kind of people we know and understand, an escape into someone else's reality. Or it may be the thriller story, or a story built around a colourful character, or a humorous story. Realistic characterization is important. So is sincerity of treatment. The exotic, the fantastic or the sordid is not wanted.

These stories can be any length from 1000 to 4000 words.

Those not interested in writing for women's magazines could try the *Sunday Post*. This, another magazine from D. C. Thompson, is designed to appeal to a wide family readership. Their guidelines say they are looking for:

> A simple story, well told, but with strong human interest reflecting the drama of everyday life and the emotions of people we know and understand, the familiar folk around us. It is more important that the reader can identify with the characters than that there should be a strong, or contrived plot. It should be written with sympathy, sincerity and understanding. If it leaves the reader with a feeling of uplift, or a lump in the throat, so much the better. We do *not* want the depressing, fantastic or sordid.

Stories to suit this market should be between 1000 and 2000 words.

Another market area for the beginner to look at is the small press. We shall look at this in some detail in Chapter 5.

2 Formulating Ideas

Awareness Wins

Many would-be authors maintain they have permanent writer's block because they lack imagination; they can never conjure that initial spark of an idea to get them going. In reality this is often due to a lack of writing experience, for writing ideas are everywhere, as I shall endeavour to demonstrate.

Often, as I browse through the shelves of my local library, I am surprised and amused at the variety of subjects authors have chosen for the themes of their books. Would you believe anybody could find sufficient raw material to compose a book entitled *Grow Your Own Hair* or to compile a work entitled *Truncheons: Their Romance and Reality*? Unlikely as they may sound, these books really do exist.

And there are a great many other specialized, narrow subjects about which people have chose to write books. If these people can produce full-length works on such trivial subjects, doesn't it follow that finding a theme for the odd filler, article or short story shouldn't present you with too much of a problem?

In my ideas book at the moment I have 13 short story ideas, 33 article ideas and 16 ideas for fillers. Some of these have been in my book for some considerable time. The truth is, once you've acquired the knack of spotting ideas you'll accumulate far more than you will ever have time to write up.

There is very little excuse for writer's block; very often would-be writers use it as a cover for laziness. Overcoming inertia can be the hardest part of the writing process and the sooner you concentrate on finding basic ideas the better. Someone once said something like 'Writing is ten per cent inspiration, and ninety per cent perspiration'. And that just about sums it up.

Having said that, this chapter is designed to make this part of the writing process as painless as possible. Select one of the following mind-joggers and mull it over in your head until something comes to you. Write down anything until thoughts gel and the words come right.

No matter what area of writing appeals to you, be it puzzles, fillers or fiction, always be alert and on the lookout for ideas.

Whatever you read, from catalogues to comics, be analytical. What did you like about the idea behind what you read? Conversely, what didn't you like? How can you avoid the same errors in your writing?

It is often easiest to write about those things for which you have strong feelings; those things which you either love or hate. Examine your own life experience: your first day at school, your first day at work, your wedding. What injustice do you feel you could help to put right?

What hobbies or interests could you write about? DIY, gardening, woodwork, needlework, cigarette packet collecting, modelling cathedrals from pipecleaners? Anything.

Do you have any pets you could write about? Is your dog a good burglar deterrent? Or does he bark at your friends and go to sleep when strangers are around? How did he react to the kennels when you went abroad for your holiday?

Think of those places you have visited recently. Regional pieces go down well with local magazines. Analyse the regional differences in culture, architecture, history, the people and their language. When you meet the people, think how their clothes could form the basis for an article, or how the local wag could be written up to form the basis for one of your fictional characters.

Do any of your friends or acquaintances have an unusual job or interest? Try to join them; experience as many new things as you can. If someone offers to take you skydiving, go, there may just be a feature article in it. Not to mention the spin-offs associated with your trip to hospital should you break a leg!

Wherever you go, whatever you do, be alert, look and listen. Record items in memory and your ideas book. Keep asking yourself the writer's watchword questions: Who? What? Why? Where? When? How?

If still nothing coming to mind try something from the following word association alphabet:

Abodes
Accidents
Addictions
Adventures
Aftermath
Agitators
Aliens
Annulments
Amphibians
Anthems

Bacteria
Balconies
Balloons
Bandages
Bassoons
Bathyspheres
Bayonets
Berserk
Butter
Buzzards

Calculus
Camaraderie
Catapults
Cauldrons
Celebrities
Champions
Charm
Chevron
Cinderella
Clover

Dances
Debris
Decadence
Decline
Delinquency
Diabolo
Disfigurement
Dragons
Dressage
Dyslexia

Earrings
Education
Egocentricity
Elizabethan
Embroidery
Enigmas
Entertainers
Episodes
Evangelism

Fashion
Feuds
Flagellation
Fleece
Floozies
Football
Forgetfulness
Fortresses
Fountains
Frontiers

Galleons
Gambling
Gardening
Gatherings
Genocide
Gestapo
Ghouls
Ginseng
Goblins
Gurus

Hijacks
Hippodromes
Hogmanay
Honeymoons
Hospitals
Hottentots
Hurricanes
Hydrophobia
Hygiene
Hypnotism

Idiots
Illusions
Immortality
Impressionists
Infanticide
Inflation
Inspiration
Islands
Isotopes
Ivory

Jade
Jealousy
Jogging
Jugglers
Juke-boxes
Jumble sales
Junk
Jury-box
Justice
Juvenile

Kaleidoscopes
Kangaroos

Kebabs
Kennels
Ketchup
KGB
Kidnapping
Kissing
Kudos
Kung fu

Lanterns
Lapidary
Legislation
Lemmings
Liquor
Litter
Loans
Lollipops
Loopholes
Lumber

Machinery
Magic
Marinade
Meringue
Mesmerism
Mines
Moonshine
Mosques
Mugging
Murder

NATO
Navigate
Nepotism
Nicotine
Noise
Nourishment
Nuclear
Nudes
Numismatics
Nymphomania

Obedience
Obesity
Ocelot
Octogenarian
Officialdom
Ointments
Olympics
Oppose
Oppression
Orang-utan

Paella
Panda
Pedigree
Pensions
Performance
Periodical
Persecution
Pesticides
Phrenology
Profession

Quadrille
Quagmire
Quakers
Quarantine
Quarry
Queen
Questionnaire
Quixote
Quorum
Quotations

Racketeering
Radiation
Ramadan
Regulations
Religion
Retirement
Rickshaws
Riots
Roulette
Rumours

Sabotage
Salesmen
Schools
Seances
Sewers
Sharks
Simulate
Skiffle
Socialism
Spring

Temptation
Terror
Thimbles

Thunder
Timber
Tobacco
Torpedo
Travesty
Turbans
Tweezers

Ulcers
Undercurrents
Unofficial
Unskilled
Unveil
Upholstery
Uranus
Urchin
USSR
Utilitarianism

Vampires
Vandalism
Vasectomy
Velvet
Venomous
Vestments
Viaducts
Vienna
Violins
Volley-ball

Waiters
Wedgewood
Whippets
Whitewash
Widgets
Witches
Wolves
Wounds
Wrinkles
Writers

Xanadu
Xanthoma
X-chromosome
Xenon
Xenophobia
Xeranthemum
Xhosa
Xiphoid
Xmas
Xylophone

Yachts
Yaks
Yarrow
Yashmaks
Yeomen
Yodelling
Yoga
Yoghurt
Youth
Yucca

Zealots
Zen
Zeppelins
Zionism
Zithers
Zodiac
Zoetropes
Zombies
Zoology
Zulus

Have any of these mind-joggers got your grey cells working yet? If they have I presume you have a note of your thoughts in your ideas book by now. Better still, you could get started right away – you can always come back to reading this when you've finished.

For those who have still to overcome inertia, here are some more stimulants.

Make it Topical

A note of topicality can often give your submission a better chance of catching an editor's eye. A reader's letter, a puzzle, a short story, an article or whatever, all are bound to have a head start over staid or stale material when slanted to suit something in vogue.

Music: A piece written around the current dance craze, or the latest top ten pop group will hold the interest of the young and the young-at-heart. Write it up to suit one of the many magazines on the stands these days.

The City: Takeover bids, and the share price index. Relate these to show how they may affect the small investor. Such an article could be slanted to suit one of the many small press business magazines available these days.

Entertainment: The off-screen romance between well-known figures of the TV soap operas of the day. How would the readers of local give-away newspaper react in their imaginary rendezvous with their favourite celebrity? Research material is no further away then your neighbours. And what better target audience than themselves – they are bound to want to read your interpretation of their views.

Sport: The cup final – what were your sports club football team doing on the great day? How did they make the most of enjoying the big event?

World news: The assassin's murder of innocent bystanders in a terrorist attack. Could this form the basis of a short story plot for your favourite small press magazine?

Topical ideas needn't just be news-related. Other slants can be suggested simply by the month of the year. Let us examine just one theme a month to get your mind working:

January: This month sees many post-Christmas sales in many high street shops and stores. Do you always get value for money on these occasions? Or do some outlets buy in cheap goods especially for the sales? What genuine bargains went for a song? Who slept on the pavement outside a famous London West End store to be first in the queue? And for how many nights? Does the incidence of shop-lifting increase on these occasions? If so, what security measures can be taken to reduce it?

February: The 14th of February is Saint Valentine's Day. Is romance still alive? What kind of people send Valentine cards, and to whom? How many married couples send cards to each other? Are men bashful when making their selection at card shops? Have you ever received an anonymous card and wondered who sent it? Have you ever sent an unsigned card? If so, what was the outcome?

March: This month sees blustery winds which can be both useful and destructive. Wind energy can be enhanced to drive traditional windmills which grind corn. Electrical power is now economically generated by the modern giant windmills in order to supplement the national grid. The Green Party is gaining ground all the time; what does the future hold for power generation by this means? Will it ever do away with the need for nuclear energy? March is an ideal time of year for wind-related sports such as sailing and gliding. What new wind sports have emerged in recent years? Photographers can put their cameras to good use now to record wind damage. How many different ways can you capture it to suit each of your local newspapers?

April: The first of the month sees April Fool's Day. Everyone loves a prank: schoolchildren, parents, teachers – even the national press have been known to run bogus stories to tease their readers. What was the silliest prank you ever fell for? What was the silliest you ever pulled? Do pranks sometimes get out of hand to cause injury or perhaps even death?

May: May Day celebrations. Will there be a May Queen at your local garden fête? And Maypole dancing? If there are they can provide good material for the photographers among you. Article writers can investigate how the festival originated, and what the Maypole is actually meant to represent. How many towns and villages still celebrate the occasion? Is it regional or national?

June: The third Sunday in the month sees Father's Day. If you write short stores think how you could angle this event to form the basis of a plot. Father's Day was first observed in 1910. Why was it introduced? There could be an article here. What about a filler or reader's letter describing the oddest Father's Day present you have ever given or received?

July: Saint Christopher the Patron Saint of Travellers is celebrated this month. Do Saint Christopher medallions actually help protect those who are out and about driving, on a bus, in a taxi, or simply out walking? If you can track down incidents where people attribute a narrow escape to their treasured medallion you could turn it into a sure-fire winner of an article.

August: Bank Holiday weekend. Do you know of any secluded spot to visit without encountering the holiday chaos? Or do you stay at home and let the maniac motorists get on with it? If you can show people how to enjoy their break in a more restful or entertaining manner you are bound to find an editor to take your idea.

September: Schools begin their new year. What is it like for the youngsters attending a new school for the first time? What of the parents' emotions? How important are the events of the first school day in forming pupil attitudes in the future? Can one isolated bad experience cause continued pupil resentment, for example? Is the wearing of school uniforms outdated? Should children be allowed freedom of expression in what they wear? Are school dinners as nourishing as they should be? How are the diabetic's and other medical dietary needs catered for?

October: Nights are drawing in and the heating season is upon us. Heating bills can be difficult to meet. What can be done to reduce them? What is the latest technology in energy-saving electronic heating programmers? The latest DIY plastic glass double glazing kits: whose are the most economic? Which is the easiest to fit? What is being done by the government to help the aged pay their heating bills? Is it enough? Fatalities among the old due to hypothermia – what can be done?

November: The 5th of November is Bonfire Night. An ideal time for the photographer. Pictures of both spectacular firework displays and disasters where bonfires have raged out of control are sure to hold local newspaper interest. Who in your area has constructed the most original Guy? A picture of it and the youngsters who made it may well interest your local give-away. What is the additional cost in your area of the extra work for the Fire Brigade and Ambulance Services at this time of year? Who foots the bill? Should the event be banned altogether to prevent associated injuries?

December: The season of rejoicing and goodwill to all men. The opportunities Christmas presents to the freelance writer are abundant. But beware the hackneyed stories that have been done to death; it is the unusual slant that will sell. Photographs of the most lavishly decorated tree in your area, or the card intended for last Christmas that arrived a year late. Are the postal services run efficiently enough? What of the charity event; what is your local Round Table doing for the under-privileged?

Time and Again

Another time-related idea-producer is the anniversary time tag. Anniversaries can easily be worked back over a set number of years: 10, 20, 50, 100, etc. They may be before or after an event. Take the Olympics, for example. You could discuss historical events or venues for future games.

The scope for this idea is enormous. Taken to its extreme you could go back six billion years to the formation of our solar system (or so some authorities estimate, at any rate).

Your filler, article, or whatever, begins: This year marks the fiftieth anniversary of so-and-so . . . or: One hundred years ago whats-his-name invented thingumajig . . .

Let us look at one dozen examples, each a decade apart:

1850: Frank S. Baldwin patented the adding machine.
Henry Wells and William Fargo started their business (at that time it was called 'American Express' – it was renamed Wells Fargo two years later in 1852).
California was admitted to the statehood in the USA.

1860: Charles Dickens wrote *Great Expectations*.
The British captured Peking.
The first horse-drawn tramway in England was introduced at Birkenhead.

1870: The GPO introduced ½d postage.
Outbreak of the Franco-Prussian War.
Degas painted his portrait of Madame Camus.

1880: Gladstone became Prime Minister for the second time.
Lew Wallace wrote *Ben Hur*.
Gilbert and Sullivan produced *The Pirates of Penzance*.

1890: The electric chair was used for the first time in the USA to execute William Kemmler (he murdered his wife).
Carlo Lorenzini, author of *Pinocchio*, died.
Britain annexed Uganda.
Opening of the first underground – City and South London line.

1900: Casey Jones died saving the lives of passengers aboard the *Cannonball*.
The relief of Ladysmith.
Tonga placed under British protection.
The Russians occupied Manchuria.
J.E. Brandenburger invented cellophane.

1910: The World War II air ace Group Captain Sir Douglas Bader was born.

Girl Guides Association founded in England by Lady Baden-Powell.
The infamous murderer Crippen was arrested.

1920: American women gained the right to vote.
Agatha Christie published her first mystery novel, *The Mysterious Affair at Styles.*
Sir Geoffrey de Havilland founded his aircraft company.
Prohibition introduced into America.

1930: Princess Margaret was born.
All Quiet on the Western Front opened.
Clyde Tombaugh discovered Pluto.
D. H. Lawrence died.
The Times Crossword appeared for the first time.

1940: Nylon stockings came onto the market.
SS *Queen Elizabeth* launched.
Raquel Welch was born.
Raymond Chandler's novel *Farewell My Lovely* published.
President Roosevelt elected for a third term in America.

1950: Labour government was returned in the General Election.
Actress Prunella Gee was born.
British steel industry nationalized.
HMS *Ark Royal* launched.

1960: The first edition of *Coronation Street* was screened.
John F. Kennedy was elected president.
The self-cleaning oven was patented.
Cassius Clay won the light-heavyweight gold medal at the Rome Olympics.
The first two-way telephone conversation was held by satellite.

New Can Be Newsworthy

The first time anything happens in the world, when it is discovered or invented, the chances are the event will be newsworthy and of interest to many people. It is also true to say that recollections of such events in following years are also capable of stimulating interest. This interest can be put to good use by the observant freelance writer to form the basis of absorbing freelance material.

Take any interest group and find a magazine covering that interest. Then find a 'first' to suit that particular outlet. Let us take a look at motoring, for example. The magazines devoted to this interest are numerous and varied: *Practical Motorist, Motor, Sports Car Monthly, Car and Car Conversion, Motor Cycle News, Motorcaravan and Motorhome Monthly,* to name but a few. And, of course, motoring does not only appeal to readers of these specialist magazines. The majority of the adult population drive. So many other general interest publications will be fair game too.

Now, how many relevant firsts covering the motoring theme can you think of? How about fifty? Too difficult do I hear you say? There's nothing to it. Try these to get your mind working:

- The first car to be used on the public highway.
- The first motor ambulance.
- The first motor bus.
- The first motorway fatality.
- The first school bus.
- The first car to be fitted with a heater.
- The first car to have air conditioning.
- The first car to be fitted with automatic transmission.
- The first car to be fitted with a radio.
- The first car to be fitted with a fridge.
- The first car to be fitted with electric lights.
- The first electric-powered car.
- The first car to have an automatic starter.
- The first all-enclosed saloon.
- The first car to be fitted with direction indicators.
- The first car to be fitted with electric windows.
- The first all-metal bodied car.
- The first car with four wheel brakes.
- The first car with four wheel drive.
- The first car to be fuel-injected.
- The first car to have headlight dippers.
- The first car to be bought on hire purchase.
- The first car to have hydraulic brakes.
- The first car to have independent suspension.
- The first production car to be capable of a top speed of 100 mph.
- The first car to be fitted with a reversing light.
- The first car to be fitted with seat belts.
- The first car to be solar-powered.
- The first car to be fitted with a syncromesh gearbox.
- The first car to be fitted with a telephone.
- The first car to be fitted with a television.
- The first car to be fitted with an anti-theft alarm.
- The first saloon car race.
- The first Formula 1 race.
- The first motor rally.
- The first magazine devoted to motoring.
- The first motor hearse.
- The first motor horse-box.
- The first time motor insurance became compulsory.
- The first articulated lorry.
- The first tanker.
- The first dumper truck.
- The first time motor racing was televised.
- The first motor show.

- The first motor caravan.
- The first motor coach.
- The first motor accident.
- The first motor accident fatality.
- The first motoring club.

See how easily ideas come once you get started? Here is a selection of a dozen other topics. See if you can find another fifty for each, whether it be for an article, a filler, or a crossword clue.

- The first typewriter was built by Italian Pellegrine Turri in 1808. The device could produce the alphabet in upper case letters only, plus four punctuation marks.
- Frenchman Louis Réard designed the first bikini in 1946. It was first publicly displayed at the Paris fashion show held on 5 July.
- The ball-point pen was invented in 1938 by a Hungarian journalist, Laslo Biro, and patented by him in Argentina in 1943. To this day, ball point pens, irrespective of manufacturer, are widely known as 'biros'.
- The first motel was the Motel Inn which opened in California on 12 December 1925. It had accommodation for 160 guests.
- The first parachute jump was made by André-Jacques Garnerin in Paris on 22 October 1797. He was released from a balloon at a height of 2230 feet.
- The first launderette opened in Fort Worth, Texas on 18 April 1934. It housed just four washing machines.
- The first safety razor was patented by its inventor King Camp Gillette on 2 December 1901. They started to roll off the production line in Boston in 1903.
- Work on the first underground railway was started at Euston Square in January 1860. The four-mile stretch of the Metropolitan line took three years to build, and was opened to passengers in January 1863.
- The first motorway was opened to public motorists in Germany in September 1921. The 6¼ mile dual-carriageway ran from Grunewold to Wannsee.
- The first successful manned space flight was made by Russian Yuri Gagarin in April 1961. His spacecraft, Vostok I, took off from Baikonur and landed safely 108 minutes later at Smelovka.
- The first jeans were made in America in 1850 by Levi Strauss. They became famous for being hard-wearing because Strauss manufactured them from tent cloth.
- The first cinema was named the Vitascope Hall and was located in New Orleans. It could house an audience of 400, and was opened on 26 June 1896.

What Luck

Superstitions stem from way back in the past, some over centuries, their origins forgotten. And yet many of them survive today in modern guises.

Most people do not like to be thought of as superstitious, but never walk under ladders, or go for that all important job interview on Friday, 13th. And just about everyone knows it's unlucky to break a mirror. But how many people know *why*? Very few, I venture to suggest. And that goes for magazine editors as much as anyone else. If you could enlighten them as to the reasons they may consider their readers would like to be enlightened too – and you will have made a sale.

Try turning one of these into an informative filler, a puzzle, or an article:

- My father used to say it was only unlucky to walk under a ladder because a pot of paint might fall on your head. But now I'm old enough to reason for myself I've come to the conclusion he made that up. The most likely explanation is that when a ladder is placed against a wall it forms a triangle: the symbol of the Holy Trinity. To walk through it would show lack of respect.
- Many people believe pearls are unlucky. The reason for this is said to be that they are likely to bring sadness because they represent solidified tears.
- Many years ago, in primitive parts, if a man saw his own reflection in a pool for example, he believed he was looking at his own soul. This was considered unharmful so long as the image remained intact. Should this image become distorted (or broken in the case of a mirror) the soul, and therefore the body, would be harmed, enough, often, to cause death. Hence the superstition that bad luck will befall anyone who breaks a mirror.
- Holly is prickly and can inflict minor wounds, so why should it be believed to be inherently lucky? Because, being evergreen, it is a symbol of enduring life, and the prickles are a deterrent to evil spirits.
- If it rains on 15 July, Saint Swithin's day, it is said it will continue to rain for forty days and forty nights. This belief dates back to the ninth century when Saint Swithin was dying. He requested to be buried outside his church in Winchester, and upon his death his wishes were respected. Many years later, the monks, as a token of respect, attempted to move his remains inside the church. But a fierce storm broke out on the day the work began (15 July) and continued unabated for forty days. This prevented the transfer taking place and was seen as a sign that the saint did not want to be moved.
- Why do some people insist upon numbering their house 12A instead of 13? It is believed by many authorities to date back to

the Last Supper, where thirteen people sat down together for the last time prior to the most famous of all historic events, the crucifixion.

- The moon has for many centuries been the source of many superstitions, not the least of which is the belief that a full moon can cause insanity. One theory for this belief is that gravitational forces influence the fluid in the brain in much the same manner that it influences the tides of our oceans. This influence was thought to have been at its height during a full moon and so tipped those close to insanity over the edge.
- Coloured cardboard cut into the shape of a horseshoe has been the symbol of good luck at many a wedding. But why should the horseshoe provide good luck? One theory is that it is made in the form of a 'C' symbolizing Christ. Another explanation is that it is a lunar symbol, forming the shape of the new moon.
- A kind of comic assault takes place at weddings when guests hurl handfuls of confetti at the happy couple. Why do they undertake this ritual bombardment? Confetti is, in fact, a substitute for grain. Originally, corn and rice were used as a fertility rite. People believed these life-giving symbols would ensure large, healthy families.
- To spill salt, as just about everyone knows, is an omen of bad luck. To counter the omen a pinch must be taken and thrown over the left shoulder. Salt is incorruptible and a preservative and so it is a symbol of immortality. To spill it would reduce its effectiveness and so allow corruption into the presence. To counter the effects a pinch of the spilled salt thrown over the left shoulder, where it was believed evil spirits lurked, would blind them and foil wicked intentions.
- Many people touch wood after making some boastful remark. But why? Pride comes before a fall they say, and so to prevent the ill-effects of a boast it is wise to touch wood as a symbol of appeasement to the gods. This is because in prehistoric times, forests and woods were believed to be the dwelling place of the gods and had been touched by them.
- One of the most common superstitious symbols is to cross fingers for luck. This is done to make the sign of the cross to invoke its protective powers to ward off bad luck that may come to mar high aspirations.

Now Where Do I Look?

The ideas we have looked at in this chapter are only a sample of the possibilities available to the enthusiastic author. There are many other groups that could jog the mind into creative action: proverbs, nicknames, common fallacies, clichés, slang, mottoes, comparisons (see Chapter 8 for some leads.) There are many other sources of ideas that you should be able to conjure up for yourself with a little thought. Spend some time in your local library – you'll be surprised how quickly ideas will form in your mind.

3 Research

Finding the Facts

Some of those who read this may think they are not going to be concerned with fact-finding as their writing speciality will always revolve around their own knowledge. But no matter what aspect of writing you are interested in, be it fillers, puzzles or articles, there is little doubt you will have to get down to some research sooner or later. Even when writing from personal experience there will sometimes be gaps in your knowledge that need to be filled.

Some people take a delight in unearthing facts and figures; others find it a chore. There are those, too, who simply do not have enough time to research *and* write.

Those whose time is limited may wish to find someone who can undertake the fact-finding for them. *The Writers' and Artists' Yearbook* (see Chapter 5) lists freelance researchers under Editorial, Literary and Production Services. These include some highly professional organizations whose charges reflect the quality of their service as well as the scope of work they are asked to perform. Other, sometimes less expensive, research services can be found in the advertisements of some specialist magazines for writers, such as *Freelance Market News*, or some of the small press literary magazines (see Chapter 5).

For the more expansive scribe with the time, a DIY approach is bound to be more rewarding – both personally and financially.

Apart from your own knowledge, material for writing can come either from other people or from published sources. Where to look will be determined to some extent by your subject. Background research for an historical short story, for example, could perhaps be solved by a delve through some books at your local library, whereas a biographical article may entail some personal interviews.

Some published sources of use to the researcher include:

- Encyclopedias
- Specialist books
- Libraries
- Catalogues
- Newspapers
- Magazines
- Press releases
- Dictionaries
- Thesauruses
- Annuals
- Atlases
- Road maps

In addition to published sources, you can obtain information from people having a knowledge of the subject of your research. This can be undertaken in person, by telephone, or by post. In my experience, personal contact generates a much better response than mailed questionnaires.

It is important always to use more than one source for your fact-finding in order to avoid inaccuracies. When I was researching some areas of this book I found various sources quoting 'facts' differently on more than one occasion. Clearly, someone was wrong. Try to ensure you never are.

Multiple sources are particularly important when relying upon personal accounts, for these can be clouded by an inflated ego and delusions of grandeur. When presented with the possibility of seeing their name in print, some people, no matter how level-headed under normal circumstances, have a tendency to overstate their involvement in a story when relating it to a researcher. The memory can also play tricks on the mind of an interviewee in the same way that it can upon the mind of the researcher. This isn't to say the deception is deliberate, but misleading it can be just the same. And should your finished submission contain inaccuracies or misleading information, an irate reader may just advise the editor of the fact – hardly an event likely to encourage that particular outlet to use your work again.

Another good reason for exploring more than one avenue is that not everyone will respond to your initial enquiry. My own experience in the field of small business is that I can expect roughly a 40 per cent response. Why the other 60 per cent don't co-operate is hard to fathom as generally my articles provide free publicity for those I write about. It is a fact all the same, and it has to be taken into account. Those that do co-operate will usually be flattered you have considered them an expert in their field and so generally will be forthcoming. But beware of digging too deep – your interviewee may not wish to give away too many secrets.

A further problem area is that of conflicting authorities. This sometimes happens when a matter of opinion can colour an interpretation of occurrences. This is particularly true of historical events because one so often has to rely on written sources. Where this occurs the choice is either to leave out controversial events altogether, or to qualify the viewpoint and be prepared to argue the stance should it ever be challenged.

Whatever the source of your information make a note of where you came by it. A record of where your fact originated will avoid inadvertent use of the same source twice. This can happen to the best of us if we allow the passage of time to dull the memory. Whenever I make a note of written sources in my ideas book I quote the name of the journal, the date of publication, and the page on which it is to be found.

Another reason for making a note of your source is that you may wish to contact the copyright owner for permission to quote a lengthy passage from it. If you don't know whom to contact, you cannot use the quote.

When exploring written material the variety is so immense it is often difficult to know where to begin. J. Whitaker publish guides to help here. Their *British Books In Print* and *Religious Books In Print* are a good starting point, as is the *Subject Guide To Books In Print* published by Bowker.

Once a title has been identified a copy of the book has to be located before research can begin. It is therefore fortunate that it is a requirement of the Copyright Act that six libraries shall each receive one free copy of every book published in the United Kingdom. The researcher can be sure of finding any British book needed in these libraries:

- The British Library (London).
- The Bodleian Library (Oxford).
- The Cambridge University Library (Cambridge).
- The National Library of Wales (Aberystwyth).
- The National Library of Scotland (Edinburgh).
- Trinity College Library (Dublin).

Another source of written material is the British Library Newspaper Library, Colindale Avenue, London. This houses a wide-ranging collection of newspapers and periodicals dating back to 1801 which are available for research purposes.

For easy reference an invaluable aid is Ann Hoffman's book *Research For Writers*, published by A. & C. Black. This work is packed with research sources and it deserves a place in any writer's bookcase. For details see Chapter 8.

But no matter where one looks there will, at times, inevitably be subjects that stump the best of us. Thriller writer Ken Royce once said he had the advice of a cat-burglar when writing his famous thriller *The XYY Man*. One certainly has to admire his ingenuity; how on earth does one get to know a cat-burglar? This is a typical example of researching a difficult subject, but when writing about something outside personal knowledge pursue them one must.

Copyright

Unearthing facts and figures from various sources, anywhere from encyclopedias to travel brochures, is perfectly legitimate research provided it is undertaken in the correct manner. There is a cliché in writing circles which says: 'Copy from one source and you will be guilty of plagiarism – copy from several sources and you will be undertaking proper research.' This may be an oversimplification of the copyright laws, but it does say something of the way in which fact-finding should be approached.

The law on copyright is a complex issue but one which needs some of your attention if you are to undertake research of any kind.

There is no international copyright law; it varies throughout the world. In Britain we are governed by the Copyright Act 1956 (with subsequent amendments). This covers literary, musical, dramatic or artistic works, sound recordings, films, television and sound broadcasts and published editions of works.

Facts, ideas, plots or themes cannot be protected by copyright; only the form in which they are expressed. If you think about it, this makes a great deal of sense for few, if any, ideas are original. If you go back over what was said in Chapter 1 regarding short story plotting you will see the method outlined is used (even if sometimes subconsciously) by a great many authors. But this plotting process is only the *idea* behind the *form*, and so may be used over and over again without any copyright being infringed.

Infringement of copyright is by the reproduction of any substantial part of a copyright work without permission. Brief sentences cannot normally be protected by copyright, for a work is only afforded protection provided it is of sufficient length to have involved the author in a certain amount of intellectual endeavour. The title of a book, therefore, cannot, under usual circumstances, be protected by copyright as it is too short to be treated as a literary work. But be careful none the less, for what constitutes a literary work is a subjective matter. The watchword should be not to copy anything unless it is for review purposes.

It is permissible to quote short passages from someone else's work provided it is for the purpose of criticism or review and so long as sufficient acknowledgement is given. A quotation of around 200 words without permission of the copyright holder is usually accepted in the trade as 'fair dealing', although it must be said the 'fair dealing' is not defined in the Copyright Act. The Society of Authors and The Publishers' Association have stated that 'fair dealing' can be considered as the use of a single extract of up to 400 words without permission provided certain criteria are met. However, as this area of the law is such a complex issue, you should always seek the advice of your intended publisher should you wish to use quotations of any kind in your work.

Whenever you make notes while undertaking research and copy the actual words used by a source you should always make a note of the fact and include all such phrases in quotation marks. This way, when you come to write up your piece, you can guard against unwittingly being guilty of copying someone else's work.

Some works may look remarkably alike in their content, but later works are not necessarily a plagiarized version of earlier works. There are many similar-looking books of babies' names for example, but provided one is not simply a copy of another no infringement has occurred.

No formalities need to be observed to copyright an original work in the United Kingdom. As soon as the work has been written, the photograph taken, or the cartoon drawn, the copyright in it belongs to the author. The manuscript/picture does not have to be printed or published to receive the benefit of protection. Nor does a piece have to be complete; a half-finished manuscript is protected in the same way as a complete, published work. No notice declaring copyright ownership need be displayed, nor is registration of any kind needed.

While no formalities need be observed by law, it is sometimes a wise precaution to have *proof* that you are the rightful copyright owner, just in case someone else should steal your work and pass it off as their own. This can be achieved quite simply. Send a copy of your manuscript to yourself by registered post, then place the unopened package in a safe place. Should a plagiarized version of your work appear, you can produce your unopened package, date stamped by the Post Office, to prove yours was the first and original version.

The period for copyright protection for the written word varies throughout many areas of the world, but in the United Kingdom it is the duration of the life of the author plus fifty years from the end of the year in which he dies. In the case of joint ownership, the work is protected during the life of the author who dies last plus fifty years from the end of the calendar year in which he dies.

Copyright protection for photographs in the United Kingdom is fifty years from the end of the year in which the photograph was first published.

Those who cannot, or do not wish, to take their own photographs to illustrate their work may choose to employ the services of someone else. In this case, if you order the original, and pay for it, the copyright belongs to you and not to the photographer.

The copyright owner of a work may assign the copyright to someone else. This must be done in writing and must be signed by, or on behalf of, the copyright owner. No other formalities are required.

Unless there are very compelling reasons for doing so, you should never sell the copyright to your work. When a publishing house buys the copyright it has the right to do with it as it will. It can edit it, shorten it or add to it. It does not have to consult you, for it is its property. It will also receive all future income from it, no matter how long it goes on selling. So, before parting with the copyright to your work you should consider its long-term value. There are some outlets, however, that rarely, if ever, buy anything but the copyright. The greetings card industry is one example. In these circumstances it is up to you to decide whether you wish to write for it at all.

Looking to the future, when the European single market begins in 1992, it is possible the United Kingdom copyright laws will be revised to bring them into line with EEC countries. The duration of copyright elsewhere in Europe currently include: 70 years in West Germany, 80 years in Spain, 64 years in France. It is likely the government will introduce legislation to extend our existing 50-year limit to 70 years.

4 *Presentation*

First Impressions Count

Most publishers receive a great number of works from authors who clearly have no idea how to present a manuscript. Some of them are hand-written, at times barely legibly. Others are submitted on odd scraps of paper – even card. Not unreasonably, the editors of national magazines do not give these sub-standard submissions a second glance. So, if your work is to be given any serious consideration it must be presented professionally.

Having said that, not all publishers like to see things presented in exactly the same way. To coin a phrase: you cannot please all of the editors all of the time. But if your manuscripts are clear and tidy and you follow some straightforward guidelines no reasonable editor will have too much cause for complaint.

The first watchword is neatness. No dust or cake crumbs. No coffee stains. No dirty fingermarks. Just straightforward clean copy.

Freelance work falls on an editor's desk by the sackful every week. From these just two or three will be chosen. Why should the editor bother to look at second-rate presentation when there is so much to choose from? Imagine yourself in the editor's chair. How would *you* react to a crisp manuscript laid alongside dog-eared toilet tissue?

All Stuck Up

When submitting a misprint or a quote there is no need to write a letter. Simply cut it out and stick it on a postcard, then add your name and address, clearly printed. Address it to your chosen market and the job's done. What could be simpler?

Hand-Written Work

Should you wish to write a reader's letter there is no need to have your work typewritten. Indeed, one could excuse an editor for passing over neatly typed letters in favour of those in manuscript. After all, they are supposed to be *readers'* letters, not the typewritten work of a professional. Not all will hold this view of course, but it is a consideration.

Letters should be neat and clear; bad handwriting simply begs to be passed over in favour of something in a legible, easy-to-follow style. When I was editor of a small press magazine I sometimes received letters from subscribers whose writing I simply could not decipher. Nor could anyone else I asked. With the best will in the world such work will never find its way into print.

Don't forget to include your address. This may sound elementary, but you do occasionally read editorial pleas for the writer of a reader's letter to come forward with their address to enable their prize to be sent on.

Try also to ensure your signature is legible. If it isn't, print your name beneath it.

Apart from readers' letters, nearly all publishers, except a handful of small presses, will not consider handwritten submissions under any circumstances. So don't try it unless contributor guidelines explicitly state handwritten work to be acceptable.

Always keep a copy of what you have sent. If it doesn't find editorial favour first time out you'll want to rewrite it to suit another market.

The Typescript

Your typewriter doesn't need to be anything special; a second-hand manual machine will do. But if you can afford it, an electric typewriter has the distinct advantage of producing neat copy irrespective of the operator's typing ability. Unlike the manual machine, each key-stroke exerts the same pressure on the ribbon to produce a professional-looking result.

Use only good quality, white bond paper of 80 gsm (grams per square metre), and type the work on one side of the sheet only. Keep a carbon; editors occasionally mislay manuscripts. Your carbon copy can be on thin bank copy paper, but not necessarily so. Many writers use whatever is conveniently to hand, including the reverse of mistyped work.

Typewriter ribbons should be black. If you use a cotton or a nylon ribbon don't use it over and over again until it produces only pale, uneven copy. Replace it. Ideally, you should use a cartridge ribbon that can be used once only.

If you have to make a correction, use a correction fluid or correction paper; never x-out your mistakes. Typing a manuscript can entail a great deal of sweat and toil but never be tempted to leave the errors rather than retype. If you make too many mistakes, scrap the page and start again.

When your piece is finished, check it thoroughly for grammatical and spelling errors. Nothing will alienate an editor more quickly than bad spelling.

Throughout your typescript be consistent in your use of capital letters, underlining, reference numbers, sub-headings, etc. If you present place names in capital letters on page 1 of your manuscript, ensure you use the same format throughout, and not underlined lower case on following pages, for example. If you begin by quoting imperial measurements don't switch to metric units halfway through. If your opening dialogue makes use of single quotation marks, ensure you don't use double quotation marks later on.

Before you sit down at your typewriter, you will need to decide what you are to call yourself. Are you going to use your real name or are you going to adopt a *nom de plume*? Many authors do use their real name, but others do not wish the outside world to know they write. The road mender simply may not wish his colleagues to know he writes romances. There is no difficulty in this. No formalities are needed in order to use a pen name. You simply choose one.

Something else you'll need to decide before typing up your manuscript is what rights you should offer. When you offer your work for the first time it will usually be on the basis of First British Serial Rights. This means you are offering a work of your own which has not been published before. This gives the publisher the right to publish it for the first time and once only in Britain. If he wishes to use it again at some time in the future he must pay for it again.

Sometimes, British publishers distribute their periodicals throughout the Commonwealth, so it is their practice to purchase First British Serial and Commonwealth Rights. This should be made clear in their acceptance letter.

Once your work has been published you may offer it again to another publisher under the terms Second British Serial Rights – if you can find a buyer, that is. Some periodicals will consider Second Serial Rights, but a great many won't. Theoretically though, you can go on selling your work indefinitely throughout Third, Fourth, Fifth Serial Rights, and so on.

Once you have sold First British Serial Rights you can still offer First Rights abroad, First North American Rights, for example. But let the editor know your work has already been published in Britain, and in which periodical.

It is rare for a publisher to ask you to sell him the copyright. But if he does, think hard – all future profit on the work will be his. If he wishes to buy the copyright, you should expect a much higher fee.

Written contracts are not usually offered for fillers, articles or short stories. When you offer work to a magazine it is accepted you are doing so on the standard terms of payment for that particular outlet. Some editors do make an offer by way of a letter, but by no means all of them. Often, the first you will know of your work being accepted will be the arrival of the cheque upon publication.

Once you have all these preliminaries sorted out you can begin typing.

When setting out a filler typescript don't use a cover sheet. Begin the main body of your work, single spaced, with your name and address in the upper right hand corner. Below that drop down two spaces and type the date. Then move across to the left-hand side of the paper and drop down two more spaces before typing the name and address of the publication to which you are making your offer. When you include the addressee's name and address and date on your manuscript it presents it as though it has been prepared exclusively for the one named publication. The disadvantage of doing this though, is that if your work is rejected you will need to retype it – or the first page in the case of lengthier pieces – before sending it out to another editor. The extra effort usually proves worthwhile.

Next, drop down four spaces and type what is on offer and add the number of words. This should be followed, two spaces down, by the rights on offer. Now drop down another four spaces and in the centre of the page type, in capital letters, the title. Everything following the title should be double spaced. Beneath it type 'by', and below that your name (or *nom de plume*).

Now for the text itself. Drop down three double-spaces and begin by indenting by five to eight spaces (whatever suits you). All paragraphs should be indented the same amount.

Always type your text using double-spacing and always leave a 35 mm margin on the left, at the top, bottom, and right side. This is to accommodate the editor's alterations and instructions to the printer.

If your filler won't fit a single sheet of paper, ensure the following pages carry, at the top of the page, the title in the left-hand corner, your surname in the centre, and the page number in the right-hand corner.

At the end of the piece, drop down three double-spaces and type a line followed by the word 'End'. Then drop down to the bottom of the sheet and type your name and address, single spaced, in the left-hand corner. (For an example of a filler manuscript see Figure 9.)

The format for any longer typescript, whether it be an article or a short story, will always be the same.

Include a cover sheet displaying the main points of the work on offer. In the top right-hand corner type your name and address. In the centre of the page type the title of the piece followed by a description of the work (whether it is an article, short story, or whatever) and below that your name (or *nom de plume*). Below that type the approximate number of words. At the foot of the page type what rights are on offer.

The next page should be headed by the title of the work, followed by your name (or *nom de plume*). The text should follow, double-spaced, with two double-spaces between paragraphs. All paragraphs should be indented by 5–8 spaces, and a 35 mm border should be left around the entire work. Where possible, include only complete paragraphs on any one page.

All following pages should contain, at the head of the paper, the title of the work, your name (or *nom de plume*) and the page number. This is because editors are busy people and the pages of your manuscript may become separated and mixed up with other papers. If your typescript is easy to identify, the situation can be retrieved without too much difficulty.

At the foot of all following pages except the very last, type 'mf' to indicate to the reader that 'more follows'. At the end of the work type a line followed by the word 'End'. Finally, type your name and address at the foot of the last page in the left-hand corner (single spaced). An example manuscript appears in Figure 10.

The format for poetry manuscripts is somewhat different from other areas of writing, for poems should always be typed in the form they are intended to appear in the final printed version. If it is to appear single-spaced then this is how the manuscript should be typed. If the final version is to have odd length indents, this is how they should appear on the typescript. The printer will print whatever he sees. It is for this reason that if your poem continues onto a second sheet of typescript without a break, you should type at the foot of the sheet 'poem continues, no break'.

In all other respects your poetry typescript can be presented in the same way as a filler.

How to Handle Illustrations

Nearly always, illustrations, whether they be line drawings, cartoons or photographs, are reproduced smaller in the published version than the original. For this reason, all illustrations intended for one submission should be produced with the same degree of reduction in mind. This is because the cost-conscious publisher will wish to reduce all of them in one process. When a hotch-potch of different-sized illustrations are presented this isn't possible and costs begin to escalate.

If you produce your illustrations on A4 paper they will con-

A. Writer,
1 Inkwell Street,
Penn,
Scribblington.

1st December 1988.

Mrs. B. Horsfall,
Writing,
87 Brookhouse Road,
Farnborough,
Hants.

An article of 200 words.

First British Serial Rights offered.

THE WRITE SLANT

by

A. Writer

Thinking up basic writing ideas can be a difficult task but nevertheless one which has to be overcome before the real business of writing can begin: no theme, no manuscript. So once an idea has surfaced in your mind, ensure you exploit it to the full by slanting it to suit as many markets as possible.

An article on the subject of writing readers' letters, for example, could be angled in several different ways to suit a number of markets. Aimed at FREELANCE WRITING AND PHOTOGRAPHY, the theme for the piece could be: "How to find the simpler avenues into print".

Figure 9

The Write Slant Writer 2.

The same readers' letters idea could be used as the theme: "How to supplement your income by writing readers' letters". Such an article could be slanted to suit the image of one of the small press business magazines such as IN BUSINESS-IN TOUCH.

Another alternative for the same topic would be to slant it to suit one of the competitions magazines such as COMPETITOR'S JOURNAL. Here, the theme could be: "Don't ignore the smaller competitions".

Here, we have been able to turn one simple idea into three quite different articles - and the same principle can be applied to just about any theme. Ideas are valuable, so don't waste them.

* * * * * * End.

A. Writer,
1 Inkwell Street,
Penn,
Scribblington.

Figure 9 continued

veniently fit together with your typescript, and so it will not be necessary for you to protect them in separate packaging. You will not be able to do this with photo illustrations though. A good standard for black and white prints is 200 mm × 150 mm, whereas transparencies should preferably be 60 mm × 60 mm.

When submitting the artwork for a crossword puzzle it is customary to include a proof of solution. If you have produced your artwork on paper the simplest way to provide the proof is by writing the solution onto a photostat copy of the frame. Those who prefer to use Bristol board for their artwork can attach tracing paper to the head of the board so the frame shows through. The solution can then be written on the tracing paper leaving the artwork untouched.

You can, of course, write the caption to your diagrams and cartoons directly onto the artwork, but ensure you write it well away from your drawing. Captions are nearly always typeset, so sufficient space has to be left for them to be inserted. Captions for photographs should be provided on a separate sheet of paper and keyed by an identification number on the back of the related print.

Number each of your illustrations uniquely, using the same number in your text. Number photographs on the back with a very soft pencil, ensuring no impression shows through to spoil the image on the front.

Despatching Your Work

A wide body of opinion in writing circles says freelance material should never be submitted under cover of a letter; that work should stand on its own merits. When it comes to filler material, such as readers' letters, jokes and the like, I wouldn't disagree with this view. But when it comes to longer pieces, such as articles and short stories, I would challenge such a stance.

When I began writing some years ago I believed a covering letter would be viewed by a busy editor as an unnecessary hindrance. But over the years I've learned that a link between writer and editor, no matter how tenuous, has to be better than nothing at all. By adopting this approach I've improved my acceptance rate, and have got to be on first name terms with some of them into the bargain. My advice is for you to do the same.

Your letter should be brief and to the point. Two sentences is all it takes:

> Here for your consideration is a 1,000-word article entitled Pot Plant Paradise. I hope you like it.

If you can find out the name of the editor and address your letter personally to him, so much the better.

A. Writer,
1 Inkwell Street,
Penn,
Scribblington,

<u>CHAIN REACTION</u>

An article by

A. Writer

800 words

FIRST BRITISH SERIAL RIGHTS OFFERED

Figure 10

CHAIN REACTION

by

A. Writer

If you are about to place a business advertisement for the first time, be warned that some of the response you receive is likely to be of a kind you didn't expect. Amongst all the genuine replies, there are bound to be one or two that promise instant wealth if you participate in their scheme. Nearly always these are chain letters.

They will try to persuade you, sometimes with a great deal of skill, how simple it is for you to make up to £625,000 in a matter of 20 to 60 days. And your only outlay for this reward is a mere £5 plus 50 envelopes and postage stamps.

Not unnaturally, this this kind of talk sounds very attractive. But can the scheme really provide the rewards it promises?

First of all, let us have a look at how the scheme is supposed to work.

Basically, all you have to do is send £5 to the first name of three that appears at the foot of the letter. Once you have done that you delete the name and move the remaining two names up so that the second name becomes the first on the list. You then add your own name so that it becomes the third name on the list.

Figure 10 continued

Chain Reaction A. Writer 4.

Take my advice, if one of these letters should fall through your letter-box, either consign it to the waste -basket or, if you are feeling public spirited, take it to your local police station.

If, after all this, you are still not convinced and insist on mailing out your £5 and 50 letters, all I ask is that you write to me letting me know when your windfall arrives. I bet I'm still waiting to hear from you in five years time.

* * * * * * End.

A. Writer,
1 Inkwell Street,
Penn,
Scribblington.

Figure 10 continued

If you have some specific qualification for writing the piece, you should say so. This will give your offering more authority:

> Here for your consideration is a 1,000-word article entitled Pot Plant Paradise. I have written the piece around my fifteen years' experience as a market gardener. I hope you like it.

Should you have a particularly involved piece in mind it is sometimes a good idea to interest an editor in the idea behind it before writing it up. It would be pointless to expend a great deal of time and effort in research and writing if the idea itself was not saleable. Write to your target editor saying why you think your piece is for him. Tell him why you are qualified to write it. If you are a cabinet-maker, for instance, tell him of your work experience and the number of years you have spent in the industry. Also, tell him of your past publishing successes, if any, even if they aren't related to the subject-matter of the idea in question. Enclose a short synopsis of your article with your letter. These will be quite enough for the editor to determine whether or not your idea deserves further investigation.

When submitting verse, do not stuff your entire life's work into the envelope in one go (for reasons I have yet to fathom this does seem to be the trait of many poets). A half-dozen is quite enough. And send either the original typescript or a good photostat copy; never a carbon copy (another trait of many spare-time poets). Constantly think: *image*.

Never staple your typescript. Secure the sheets together with a paper clip. Try not to fold your work but mail it flat. If you have included a photograph or illustration, use a card-backed envelope. Do not use secondhand envelopes; battered and torn packaging covered in correction fluid and sticky tape never impressed anyone.

When sending out your work always include a stamped, self-addressed envelope for its return should it prove unsuitable. Editors receive a great many speculative submissions, and they cannot be expected to foot the bill for returning work they have not asked to see.

When writing seasonal or anniversary pieces you will need to consider the timing of your submission. A piece about the origins of Christmas puddings submitted in the middle of December will arrive too late to be considered. The copy for a Christmas edition of a monthly magazine could have been selected as early as September. I suggest the following to be the minimum lead times you should allow:

Weekly publications – 2 months
Monthly publications – 3 months
Quarterly publications – 6 months

Some editors respond quickly to speculative submissions, some do not. This state of affairs can create problems, for as time passes and you don't hear anything you are left wondering whether you simply have a slow-coach editor on your hands, or whether your manuscript has gone astray in the post. The temptation here is to telephone or write to enquire whether it arrived. But you should resist over-eagerness if you are to avoid irritating your target editor. Some publications will even tell you this in their contributor guidelines. The quarterly magazine *Evergreen*, for example, state in their guide for contributors:

> Please do not write or telephone enquiries concerning the fate of your material until at least three full months have elapsed since you submitted it. Material is invariably returned without further consideration to an over-zealous contributor.

I always wait three months before querying weekly or monthly magazines and six months for quarterlies.

5 Know Your Market

Commercial Magazines and Newspapers

No self-respecting writer can afford to do without detailed market research, no matter what area of writing is of interest to him. I've made this statement before but the point simply cannot be overemphasized. Even if you've once been familiar with a journal but have not seen a copy for a while, it is important to get up to date before attempting to write for it. Magazines come and go, and editorial requirements change with the times as well as with new management. By the time you read this book a number of the markets I have mentioned could have changed dramatically or could have ceased publication altogether.

Decide which magazines you would like to write for and study several recent issues. Examine length, style, treatment. Note paragraph and sentence length, and the average length of words used. Who is the typical reader? Young, old, middle-aged? Examine not just the editorial matter but the advertisements too. What do they tell you about the kind of person buying the magazine? Once you have identified who it is, write in a style and at a level to suit him or her.

When contemplating writing lengthier pieces, always send for a copy of your target magazine's contributor guidelines. These can be very detailed at times, and can save a great deal of wasted effort in producing the wrong slant.

Most people are aware of the national glossy weekly magazines lining the shelves of their local newsagents, but how many know about the small specialist magazines designed for an enthusiast market? The number of magazines catering for minority interest groups is amazing. Did you know there are magazines devoted to football referees, hospital patients, bee-keeping, embroidery and rambling?

There are thousands of magazines which most people don't know exist. It is usually only those who develop the special interest catered for who know about them. But if you can track them down you could turn them into a paying outlet for your work. Here are 100 examples of lesser-known magazines which you can get from your newsagent:

A La Carte
Antique Clocks
Antique Collector
Arthritis News
Art Monthly
Arts Express
Athletics Weekly

Baptist Times
Basketball Monthly
Bee World
Bicycle
Black Belt International
British Birds

Camping and Caravanning
Canal and Riverboat
Caravan
Cat World
Caterer and Hotelkeeper
Challenge
Christian Music
Church News
Climber
Clocks
Competitor's Journal
Cooks Monthly
Country
Country Living
Country Sport
Country Walking
Coarse Fisherman
Cue World
Crops Weekly

Dance Theatre Journal
Dancing Times
Descent
Design
Director
Diver
Driver

Embroidery
Exploring the Supernatural
Essex Countryside

Farmlife
Farming News
Farmer's Guardian
First Down
Footloose

Garden Answers
Gardening News
Golden Age
Good Food Retailing
Good Ski Guide
Grower
Guitarist

Handgunner
Headlight
Home Farm

Importing
Interior Design
Interzone

Jam

Kennel Gazette
Key Ideas
Knit and Stitch

Machine Knitting Monthly
Machine Knitting News
Marketing Week
Motive Power

Office Secretary
On the Move
Outdoor Action

Parks and Sports Grounds
Performance Bikes

Railway Magazine
Rambler
Riding
Running Magazine

Salmon
Sea Breezes
Seascape
Shooting News
Snooker Scene
Small Gardens
Squash World
Stock

Target
The Craftsman
The Grocer
The Vegan
Teacher
Traditional Woodworking
Transport Week

Vegetarian

Waterways World
What Boat
Workout
World of Knitting

Yoga Today
You and Your Vet
Yesterday

This list alone should convince you of the massive number of potential outlets that are open to freelance writers. There is room for just about everyone; it's merely a question of knowing where to look.

To assist you with your market research you should consider including one of the following reference works on your bookshelf. They should not be thought of as a *substitute* for an actual examination of your target publications of course, but they can cut out a great deal of work by pointing you in the right direction initially.

Writers' and Artists' Yearbook. Published by A. & C. Black (Publishers) Ltd, annually. More than 600 British and 200 overseas magazines and newspapers are covered by the *Yearbook*, giving editorial requirements and rates of pay. It also lists outlets for poetry, music, books, plays and broadcasting. Other lists cover literary agents, art, picture libraries, literary prizes, societies and editorial services. There are also some excellent articles covering: magazines, poetry, International Standard Book Numbering, vanity publishing, theatre, TV, radio, agents, art, music, prizes, clubs, research, copyright, tax, libel, social security, publishing agreements, public lending rights, manuscript preparation, word processing, proof correction and translations. The price of this guide at the time of writing was £5.95, and available at bookshops. In the event of difficulty, write to the publishers:

A. & C. Black (Publishers) Ltd
35 Bedford Row,
London,
WC1R 4JH

The Writer's Handbook, edited by Barry Turner. Published by the Macmillan Press Ltd, annually. This recently introduced yearbook provides an interesting alternative to the *Writers' and Artists' Yearbook*. It gives the editorial requirements of magazines and newspapers, as well as their circulation figures and rates of pay. It also lists publishers, literary agents, broadcasters, theatres, associations, research services and literary prizes and awards. On top of all this there are articles on the subjects of contracts, critics, public lending rights, poetry, literary agents, newspapers, broadcasting, theatre, copyright, tax and word processing. The price of this guide at the time of writing was £5.95, and available at bookshops. In the event of difficulty write to the publishers:

The Macmillan Press Ltd,
4 Little Essex Street,
London,
WC2R 3LF

Freelance Market News. An A4 newsletter published eleven times a year and available on subscription only at £17.50 p.a., or £9.75 for six issues. The address is:

Freelance Press Services,
5–9 Bexley Square,
Salford,
Manchester,
M3 6DB

This is an invaluable aid to all freelance writers of all levels of writing ability for it is devoted to providing up-to-date markets, both British and overseas. It covers a broad spectrum of publications from small press to national glossies and gives their editorial requirements. There is also a feature devoted to competitions.

Free Magazines and Newspapers

A vast potential outlet, often overlooked by the freelance writer, is the give-away newspapers. At one time the freebies were thought of purely as an advertising medium filled with nothing but a sea of classified and display advertisements. But over the years their image has improved until now many are a good read, and free into the bargain. Very often they contain local news, general interest articles, horoscopes, crossword and other puzzles, as well as the expected advertising content.

Despite all this, the belief persists in some quarters that free newspapers are thrown into the waste bin without being read. But independent research has shown that free newspapers are read by all who receive them and the average time spent reading give-aways is very nearly 25 minutes. Surveys have also shown that of its readership 57 per cent read half or more of each issue.

Research undertaken by members of the Association of Free Newspapers indicates that 95 per cent of households now receive copies of free newspapers – this is twice as many as receive paid-for weekly newspapers. Of these people as many as 91 per cent read what they receive. Another way of saying this is that a total of 75 per cent of all UK adults now regularly read a free newspaper, which is significantly more than read a national daily newspaper.

Readership of free newspapers is high across all age and socio-economic groups, with roughly the same proportion of men and women.

In 1987 there was a total of around 965 free newspaper titles distributing 40 million copies weekly. The Association of Free Newspapers has within its membership just under half of these; in 1987 this amounted to 452 titles distributing 22.8 million copies weekly.

In addition to free newspapers, recent years have also seen a steady growth in the number of free magazines. In 1987 the Association of Free Magazines and Periodicals saw the publication of 485 titles within its membership.

Clearly, the market opportunities free newspapers and magazines offer the freelance are enormous. So the next time a freebie falls through your letter box, examine it carefully to see how you could exploit it as an outlet.

Those enthusiastic enough to explore this market to its ultimate could consider making contact with the Association Of Free Newspapers for a copy of their directory entitled *A-Z of Britain's Free Newspapers and Magazines*. This provides postcode data and area distribution maps, together with circulation figures for almost 50 per cent of the country's free newspapers and magazines. While the directory would be invaluable in tracking down free periodicals surrounding your area, it has to be said that its cost at £30 would be prohibitive to all but the dedicated. However, for those keen enough, the directory can be obtained from:

Association of Free Newspapers Ltd,
Ladybellegate House
Longsmith Street,
Gloucester,
GL1 2HT.

Small Press Magazines

What is a small press magazine? Definitions from different sources vary, but I would define a small press magazine as one produced by the efforts of just one or two individuals, or perhaps the members of a writers' circle, and one which is not to be found in the high street newsagents. Such magazines are usually low circulation and often non-profit-making.

Small press magazines are mostly considered to be either 'literary' or 'enthusiast'. (There are also those that purport to be the former but are in fact a poor substitute for the latter.) The beginning writer would be well advised to concentrate his efforts on the enthusiast-style magazines. Competition for publication within the pages of the literary publications can be very fierce – certainly just as fierce as the competition experienced by submissions aimed at the nationals – because of the prestige associated with being published by such outlets. They are often grant aided by Arts Councils, which in itself sets a seal of approval upon the standard of works published. This is particularly true of outlets for poetry.

Many of the enthusiast-style magazines run competitions offering cash prizes. This is particularly good news for those whose main interest lies in writing fiction, for national markets for short stories (except for romances) are few and far between. But the watchword for all small press magazines is the same as for the nationals: select your market with care and follow the rules to the letter. I used to edit a small press magazine that ran competitions and I can testify to the fact that many aspiring writers do not undertake market research. And sometimes, even when entrants did read the rules, they flagrantly disregarded them. Some competitions merely require entries to fall within a maximum length – but even this can be ignored. One competition I ran specified a maximum length, but more than 10 per cent of entries went over it, some by as much as twice the allowance length. Needless to say, they went onto the reject pile without being read. Submissions that contravene the rules of entry, no matter in how small a way, will not be considered, irrespective of how good they are.

Small press magazines do not only run competitions, of course. Many offer a regular platform for all manner of material. It is just that competitions pay better. Indeed, some small press magazines don't pay for work other than competitions, so it is important for you to check first.

The main problem the beginner will have with this market is finding the magazines in the first place. Small press usually means circulation is low and distribution limited. Sometimes they form part of a writers' club and are distributed solely among its members. Others, often run by individuals, are marketed by word of mouth by its producers and subscribers, and via the mail through selective advertising. Fortunately, this point has been recognized and as a result the following directories have emerged:

Privately Published Periodicals. Compiled and published by G. Carroll. This, itself a small press publication, lists over 100 magazines, their editorial requirements and, where appropriate, rates of pay. The guide costs £3.00 including postage and is available from:

G. Carroll,
11 Shirley Street,
Hove,
East Sussex,
BN3 3WJ.

Small Presses and Little Magazines of the UK and Ireland. Compiled by Peter Finch. This directory is published by the Welsh Arts Council and lists over 250 periodicals. It doesn't provide editorial requirements, but that is not necessarily a bad thing. As we have said, there is no substitute for an actual study of the publications for which you aim to write. The directory costs £1.25 post paid, and is available from:

Oriel,
53 Charles Street,
Cardiff,
CF1 4ED.

6 Record-Keeping

Who Has What?

As soon as you begin to write you will need to keep accurate records of your output and of the markets to which you offer it. Otherwise you'll lose track of where your manuscripts are and how long they have been out on offer.

You will need to know what is out and to whom, both to ensure none of your work goes astray and to ensure you don't offer a particular piece of work to the same outlet again following a rejection. You should know whether or not you need to write enquiring about an editorial decision, or for that matter, whether you need to chase an overdue cheque.

My system comprises just one standard record sheet, which I find quite adequate. The sheet has seven columns. In the first I write a description of the work offered. In the following four columns I enter where the work has been offered and the date it was sent to each publication. The first of these columns is for the original target publication. If the work is not accepted by that market I move on to the next column, and so on. The sixth column tells me who accepted my offer and when. In the seventh column I enter the fee received. Note that I say the fee *received* and not the fee *offered*. Just because your work has been accepted, even by a well-established publication, don't automatically assume you will get paid. The majority of periodicals are run in a business-like manner and pay up on time, but extracting money from a few badly organized concerns is more difficult than robbing the Bank of England. Needless to say, those that give trouble are to be avoided in the future. For this reason I only enter up column seven when I have actually been paid. This way I can keep track of who owes me money. For a typical record sheet see Figure 11.

As a general principle no news is good news; many editors return rejected manuscripts quite quickly while hanging on to those they are either undecided about or are sure they will use when the right slot appears. This is not always true, of course, particularly of the quarterlies, but in my experience it is so in the majority of cases.

I go through my submission list about once a month to check outstanding editorial decisions. If I haven't heard anything for a while (three months for weeklies and monthlies, and six months for quarterlies) I send a polite letter of enquiry addressed personally to the editor. This reads something like this:

Dear Mr Typefinger,

On 10th June 1988 I offered for your consideration a 1,000-word article entitled 'Going Places'. As I've not heard from you perhaps you would be kind enough to let me know whether or not you received the manuscript, and if so whether or not it is still under consideration. SAE enclosed for your reply.

Many thanks.
Yours sincerely,

A. Writer.

You cannot expect to receive acceptance letters or rejection slips for everything you send out, of course. I've never heard of an editor issuing a notification either way for a reader's letter, for example. The first you'll know about your letter being accepted will either be when it appears in print or when your payment arrives. So how long should you wait before you can assume your work has been rejected? How do you know when you can safely offer unaccepted letters elsewhere? No one can be dogmatic about this, of course, but I would allow six months to go by before resubmitting work previously on offer to weeklies or monthlies, and twelve months for quarterlies.

Whenever I look over my records for outstanding editorial decisions I also check for overdue payments. If I find any fees still to be paid two months after the item appeared in print I send an invoice. This is of very simple format but usually it is enough to elicit payment. Here is an example:

INVOICE NO. 23

Article of 1,000 words entitled Going Places, published in the January 1988 edition of *Soapbox News* for an agreed fee of £40.

Should I hear nothing after the issue of the invoice I ring the editor concerned. In all but two instances in my writing life this has

ITEM	OFFERED TO:				PUBLISHED BY	FEE RECEIVED
Letter re plastic cup	Weekend 5/5/88					
"Blue Is The Sky" (poem)	Outposts 7/5/88					
"Hold Up" (s. story)	Weekend 9/5/88 R	Revue 11/8/88 R	Sunday Post 14/10/88			
"Sounds Familiar" (article)	Comp Journal 12/5/88				C.J. 17/9/88	£7-50 7/10/88
Letter re credit cards	Weekly News 17/5/88				W.N. 4/8/88	Pen & pencil set 3/9/88
Joke about beer	Weekly News 24/5/88				W.N. 20/8/88	£2-00 15/10/88
Cartoon about trumpet	In Business 1/6/88					
Letter re braces	Chat 7/6/88					
Limerick about skier	Weekly News 14/6/88					
"Gone Fishing" (s. story)	Golden Years 20/6/88 R	Western Morning News 10/9/88				

Figure 11

been enough to elicit payment. In the other two instances I have cut my losses by never submitting work to those non-paying outlets again. I also advised writers' magazines so they could spread the word to warn their readers.

Keeping Accounts

As soon as you begin to make money from your scribblings the Inland Revenue will wish to share in your good fortune. For this reason it is essential you keep accurate details of both income and expenditure associated with your writing.

To begin with, when it is likely your writing output will be relatively small, you will probably be assessed under Case VI of Schedule D of the Income and Corporation Taxes Act 1970. In this case *bona fide* business expenses can be deducted in arriving at taxable income, but, if your expenses exceed your income, your loss can only be set against the profit from future isolated transactions, or other income assessable under Case VI.

Once you have gained some experience and your output has increased it may be possible to argue that, while your writing may be part-time, it is a profession none the less. In this case you will be assessed under Clause II of Schedule D of the Income and Corporation Taxes Act 1970. In this case, if your expenses exceed income, the loss can either be carried forward and set against future income from your freelance writing or set against other income subject to tax in the same year.

But enough of all this, in either case if your derive any income from freelance writing you will need to submit details to the Inland Revenue. So remember to keep a note of *all* your related expenditure in order to offset it against your earnings. And try to keep all associated receipts.

Any expenses incurred to enable you to undertake your writing are likely to be legitimately offset against your income for tax purposes. So ensure you make a note of everything. Here is a checklist of deductable items:

- Any expenses in employing secretarial, typing or research services.
- Telephone charges, postage, stationery, pens, pencils, paper, typewriter ribbons, film, photographic processing expenses, maintenance and insurance of your typewriter, photocopier and other office equipment.
- Magazines and books used for market and subject research.
- Travel expenses, hotels, fares, car running expenses including repairs, petrol, oil, garaging, cleaning, parking, road tax, depreciation, insurance, AA/RAC membership.

- Capital allowances for your typewriter, desk, photocopier, filing cabinet.
- The proportion of heating and lighting bills associated with the room used to undertake your writing activities.
- Subscriptions to professional societies and associations.
- Accountancy charges.

Your accounting system needn't be complicated; to begin with a simple 'in' and 'out' book is all you will need. On the left-hand page you should record details of all your income and the date the income was realized. On the right-hand page you should record details of all expenses incurred while undertaking your writing activities. Typical examples are shown in Figure 12.

If your earnings from writing exceed a certain amount you will become liable for VAT and must register with HM Customs as a taxable person. The amount changes from time to time but as I write this the amount is £23,600 annually, or if your income exceeds £8,000 in any one quarter. A call to the Customs office will give the up-to-date figure. If your earnings fall below the current limit you will be exempt from registration.

However, I venture to suggest that most who read this book, unless they are singularly gifted or extremely lucky, will not earn sufficient to worry themselves about registration. If you are fortunate enough to be in the money, you could cheerfully employ the services of an accountant – and smile all the way to the bank.

INCOME

DATE	DETAILS	AMOUNT
3/9/88	Letter to Weekly News (pen & pencil set)	in kind.
7/10/88	Article in Competitors' Journal	7-50
15/10/88	Joke in Weekly News.	2-00
1/11/88	Article in In Business	16-00
14/11/88	Letter in Weekend	10-00
2/12/88	Aritcle in Mother	120-00
15/12/88	Letter in Best	5-00
20/12/88	Filler in Writing Magazine	3-00

Figure 12a

EXPENSES

DATE	DETAILS	AMOUNT
1/5/88	Postage stamps	3-60
4/5/88	Envelopes	2-50
7/5/88	Fares to British Museum	3-20
9/5/88	Magazines for research: Best	40
	Countryman	1-10
	Do It Yourself	1-10
	Evergreen	1-75
	Scots Magazine	55
17/5/88	Photocopies	1-20
20/5/88	Pencils	80
28/5/88	80g. typing paper	6-10

Figure 12b

7 Keeping in Touch

Magazines For Writers

All freelance writers should keep in touch with market trends and news. One of the simplest ways of doing this is by subscribing to one or more of the specialist magazines devoted to the subject. In addition to the nationally distributed commercial publications many others roll off small presses. Some of these are largely designed as a platform for writers' work, while others offer advice on the writing process itself. In my review here I have included only those small press magazines which offer guidance to writers rather than just a potential outlet for their work.

Writers' Monthly. Published monthly and available on subscription only at £33.50 per annum from:

The Writer Ltd,
18–20 High Road,
London,
N22 6DN.

This is a professionally presented glossy A4 format magazine, which will be of interest to those at all levels of writing ability and experience. There are articles to suit both the absolute beginner as well as the seasoned author of a dozen books or more. In addition to feature articles, regular spots include a letters page, competitions (with worthwhile cash and other prizes), new and existing markets analysed, an update file giving editorial changes, book news, features on writers' circles countrywide, reviews of small press output, literary news. A well-presented magazine having something to interest all.

Freelance Writing and Photography. Published quarterly and available on subscription only at £7.50 per annum from:

Freelance Writing and Photography,
Victoria House,
Victoria Road,
Hale,
Cheshire,
WA15 0RB.

While this was once thought of as a small press magazine, I doubt many would view it in this light today. Since changing hands a couple of years ago it has grown in both content and quality. A nicely produced A4 size magazine containing articles of interest to a large cross-section of writers. The articles offer advice on all areas of freelance writing and photography. It also contains writer profiles, book reviews and readers' letters. The house style tends to be 'literary' and so will be of interest to the more serious writer.

Writer's Digest. Published monthly and available on subscription at £22.00 per annum, or £1.95 for a sample copy, from:

Freelance Press Services,
5–9 Bexley Square,
Salford,
Manchester,
M3 6DB.

While this is an American publication, 90 per cent of its content is relevant to the British writer. It is a glossy covered A4 format magazine of interest to writers of all levels of ability. It contains articles on most areas of writing including construction, technique, style, ideas and American markets. It also uses readers' letters and writer profiles.

The Writer. Published monthly and available on subscription at £22.00 per annum, or £1.95 for a sample copy, from Freelance Press Services at the above address. Another American journal of interest to the British writer. This glossy covered A4 format magazine is suitable for writers of all abilities. It contains letters to the editor, articles on many aspects of freelance writing, and American markets.

Success. Published six times per year and available on subscription of £10 per annum, or £5.50 for six months. The address is:

Success,
17 Andrews Crescent,
Peterborough,
PE4 6XL.

Founded in 1968, this is another well-established small press magazine. Regular features include an editorial, readers' letters, news of writers' circles and conferences, literary competition news, market news, book and poetry reviews.

Writing. Published three times per year and available on subscription of £3.00 per annum, or £1.25 for a single issue. The address is:

Writing,
87 Brookhouse Road,
Farnborough,
Hants,
GU14 0BU.

This is a small press magazine offering both a platform for amateur writers' work as well as articles of guidance. Also contains an editorial, readers' letters, magazine and book reviews. A well-thought-out magazine founded in 1959.

Writing Today. Published quarterly and available on subscription of £5.85 per annum, or £1.50 for a single issue. The address is:

Writing Today,
109 Redlam,
Blackburn,
BB1 1UN.

A relatively recent addition to the small press scene, this is a nicely designed, well-printed, A5 format magazine containing articles on all areas of freelance writing. Other features include an editorial, magazine and book reviews, readers' letters and market news.

Writing Clubs and Associations

Another way to keep in touch with news of events and current trends is to join a writers' circle. if you do not know of one in your area, you would do well to obtain a copy of Jill Dick's *Directory of Writers' Circles*. This is arranged alphabetically listing Writers' Circles and similar groups throughout the United Kingdom and Eire. The Directory is published by Laurence Pollinger Ltd, and costs £3.00 including postage. It is available direct from its compiler, Jill Dick, at:

'Oldacre',
Horderns Park Road,
Chapel-en-le-Frith,
Derbyshire,
SK12 6SY.

Given below are details of four organizations I believe could benefit the beginning writer. There are numerous other writing groups in existence, but I haven't included those I consider to be more suited to the experienced professional.

The British Amateur Press Association, as the name implies, is designed for an enthusiastic amateur membership. The Association was founded in 1890 under a different title. The present title was introduced in 1910.

The aims of the society are stated to be: 'To promote the fellowship of writers, artists, editors, printers and publishers and other craftsmen/women and to encourage them to contribute to, edit, print and publish, *as a hobby*, magazines, books and literary works produced by letterpress or other process.' The Association is non-sectarian, non-political and non-profit-making.

For an annual fee members receive, every two months, what is known as the 'bundle'. This is the term used for the envelope containing official news and publications, plus a selection of private magazines produced by members. The 'bundle' also contains the *Members' News Bulletin* giving membership news and other up to date information.

In addition to the 'bundle' being issued six times per year, members also receive the Association's official magazine *The British Amateur Journalist*. This currently appears three times a year. Non-members can order an annual subscription to this magazine for a fee of £2.00 including postage.

Membership of the Association is open to anyone who pays the appropriate annual subscription, which at the time of writing was as follows:

Adult membership – £4.50 p.a.
Junior membership (under 18s) – £3.00 p.a.

Special rates are available for family groups, residing at the same address, subject to only one 'bundle' being sent to that address at each mailing:

First adult member – £4.50 p.a.
Other adult, each – £2.00 p.a.
Children, under 18, each – £1.00 p.a.
When both parents are members, membership for children under 16 years of age is free.

An application form contained within an informative booklet can be obtained from:

Mr L. E. Linford,
British Amateur Press Association,
78 Tennyson Road,
Stratford,
London,
E15 4DR.

For a small press group to have stayed in business for nearly 100 years is a feat worthy of praise and of your support.

The Association of Little Presses was founded in 1966 by a small group of individuals running their own little presses with a view to self-help and encouragement. Over the years their organization grew, but even today it is run entirely by voluntary efforts. It is also grant-aided by Greater London Arts.

ALP members produce everything from comics and cookery hints to novels and books on naval history. They publish psychic studies, games, puppetry, travel, religion – anything.

Designed primarily to assist small presses and magazines, as well as individuals looking to publish their own work, the information membership provides can also be of benefit to individuals seeking an outlet for their work. The Association represents over 250 publishers and associations throughout Britain, and as small presses and their magazines account for over 80 per cent of all new published poetry in this country, this organization is likely to be of interest to the enthusiastic poet.

The Association also organizes numerous book fairs and exhibitions all over the country each year.

Membership costs £7.50 per annum. For this you will receive a quarterly magazine entitled *Poetry and Little Press Information* (PALPI). Non-members can purchase this for £3.00 for four issues, post paid. The magazine gives details of recent little press and poetry publications.

Also included in the membership is the *ALP Newsletter*, published from time to time, which includes general small press information, printing and distribution advice.

You will also receive a copy of the sizeable annual *Catalogue of Small Press Books in Print*. This is also available to non-members at £2.00 plus 55p postage. The catalogue gives details of little presses in print and their output.

For further details of membership write to:

Bob Cobbing,
Coordinator,
Association of Little Presses,
89A Petherton Road,
London,
N5 2QT.

The Penman Club is another organization worthy of attention. It is a club designed to suit those of varied literary ability, both published and unpublished.

For the beginning writer the club offers a criticism service as well as market suggestions. Both new work and work having found unfavourable editorial response can be submitted for appraisal. All criticism and advice is given by published authors and journalists, free of charge to members. If your work is not up to publication standard you will be told so and advised where you are going wrong. You will also be provided with suggestions to correct your mistakes. This service is particularly useful to the beginning writer because handwritten work will be accepted for criticism. The Club also offers a typing service for its members for an extra fee.

If you are already a selling writer but are undergoing a sticky patch the Club offers help here also. And for those selling regularly there is a special department designed to help broaden market awareness.

Members are entitled to make use of a wide choice of reference works from the Club's library service. Upon joining, new members are sent a list of books available; each of which when borrowed may be kept for personal use for a period of two weeks. The only charge made for the loan of books is to cover postage costs.

The General Secretary keeps a list of all those members wishing to make contact with pen friends, and will make suitable introductions when requested to do so.

Upon enrolment, each new member is sent a 10-lesson fiction writing course covering all elements of the craft from basic plotting right through to typing up the final manuscript and submitting it to a publisher.

All these benefits can be had for a once-only enrolment fee of £3.00 plus an annual subscription as follows:

1 year – £5.25
3 years – £15.00
5 years – £20.00

Those wishing to join should write to the General Secretary for an enrolment form at:

The Penman Club,
175 Pall Mall,
Leigh-on-Sea,
Essex,
SS9 1RE.

Finally, we come to the *Freelance Press Services Bureau*. Don't be put off by the professional-sounding name, for membership is suitable for most levels of writing ability.

Their General Advice Bureau offers assistance of any kind either by telephone or by letter. They hold a reference library of many books and directories to enable them to answer queries both on the home and overseas markets.

They can give advice on publishers' offers and agreements, and can act as intermediary when you have problems with extracting fees from reluctant payers.

The Bureau has contacts in many overseas countries and can put you in touch with collaborators, or simply find you pen friends abroad.

Membership entitles you to a 10 per cent discount on any one of around 150 books for writers and photographers they keep in stock.

In order to assist you in gaining access to events of interest, you will be provided with 'Press' car stickers and a 'Freelance Press Card' bearing your photograph.

Annual membership also entitles you to receive their magazine *Freelance Market News* each month (for details of this publication see Chapter 5).

Twelve months' membership to the Bureau costs £28.00 and an enrolment form can be obtained from:

Freelance Press Services,
5–9 Bexley Square,
Salford,
Manchester,
M3 6DB.

8 Books to Help the Writer

Getting The Words Right

No matter what area of writing interests you the following reference works will help you select the right work for each and every occasion, and just as importantly, will ensure your spelling is accurate too.

The Concise Oxford Dictionary. Published by Oxford University Press. No freelance writer should be without a dictionary, and this one is as good as you'll need.

Roget's Thesaurus of Synonyms and Antonyms. Originally compiled by Peter Mark Roget, and later revised and enlarged, first by John Lewis Roget, and later by Samuel Romilly Roget. My edition was published by The Number One Publishing Co. Ltd, in 1972. An invaluable aid for all areas of writing whenever you are stuck for an alternative word.

The Quickway Crossword Dictionary. Compiled by Colonel H. W. Hill. First published by Frederick Warne and Co. Ltd, in 1953. Groups words alphabetically in lengths of two to eight letters. A must for all puzzle compilers.

Words to Rhyme With. Compiled by Willard R. Espy. First published by Macmillan Press in 1986. Contains 80,000 words that rhyme, to help the writer of verse.

Formulating Ideas

The following books cover those areas looked at in Chapter 2, as well as a number of new ones. Wherever I have quoted a publication date I have used the date first published; in many instances later editions may be available.

Dictionary of Dates. Seventh edition (1986) revised by Audrey Butler. First published by J. M. Dent and Sons Ltd, in 1911. A chronology of events from 30,000 BC to the present day. Anything from cigars to dynamite, X-rays to suicide – it is all here.

Encyclopaedia of Dates and Events. Compiled by L. C. Pascoe, A. J. Lee and E. S. Jenkins. First published by The English University Press as one of their Teach Yourself Books in 1968. Entries begin at 5000 BC and finish at 1950.

The Book of Days. Compiled by Bob Monkhouse. First published by Arrow Books Ltd, in 1981. Lists events for all 365 days of the year, covering a great many years.

The Book of Days. By Anthony Frewin. First published by William Collins Sons and Co. Ltd, in 1979. Lists events for the 365 days of the calendar.

The Shell Book of Firsts. Compiled by Patrick Robertson. First published by Ebury Press and Michael Joseph Ltd, in 1974. Around 6000 'firsts' are listed, from the first electric light bulb to the first teddy bear.

A Book of Superstitions. Written by Raymond Lamont Brown. First published by David and Charles in 1970. A collection of superstitions of all kinds from all ages and many countries.

The Encyclopedia of Superstitions. Edited by Christina Hole. First published by Hutchinson and Co. Ltd, in 1948. This book explains the origin and meaning of superstitions of today and yesterday, and how ancient beliefs have been adapted to modern living.

Superstitions. Written by Peter Haining. First published by Sidgwick and Jackson Ltd, in 1979. Covers a vast range of beliefs with examples, and explains their origin.

A World of Proverbs. Written by Patricia Houghton. First published by Blandford Press in 1981. Anything from 'A fool and his money are soon parted' to 'All Hallows moon, witches soon', they are all here in this book.

The Oxford Dictionary of English Proverbs Third edition. Compiled by William George Smith and edited by F. P. Wilson. This edition was published by Oxford University Press in 1970. The proverbs vary from the cautious wisdom of our forefathers to 'Take counsel of one's pillow' to the modern maxim 'If it works it's obsolete'.

The Concise Oxford Dictionary of Proverbs. Edited by John Simpson. First published by Oxford University Press in 1982. Proverbs date back centuries, as this book demonstrates so well. 'If the cap fits wear it': 1600; 'Don't teach your grandmother to suck eggs': 1707; 'There's no fool like an old fool': 1546.

Nicknames. Written by Vernon Noble. First published by Hamish Hamilton in 1976. This is a compilation of nicknames for people, places and events. Romeo, pommy, nosey and grog, are just a few of the common nicknames to be given an airing in this interesting book.

The Dictionary of Historic Nicknames. Compiled by Carl Sifakis. First published by Facts on File Publications in 1984. A treasury of more than 7500 famous and infamous nicknames from world history.

A Dictionary of Common Fallacies. Compiled by Philip Ward. First published by The Oleader Press in 1978. The belief that lightning never strikes twice in the same spot is discredited, as are a great many more commonly held beliefs.

The Dictionary of Clichés. Compiled by James Rogers. First published by Ward Lock Ltd, in 1986. For better or for worse this book contains over 2000 of the English language's most over-used expressions.

The Joy of Clichés. Written by Nigel Rees. First published by Macdonald and Co. (Publishing) Ltd, in 1984. At the end of the day this book, above all others, will help to give your writing sparkle where all others have failed – indeed, everything you always wanted to know about clichés but were afraid to ask.

A Concise Dictionary of English Slang – Third edition. Compiled by B. A. Phythian. This edition published by Hodder and Stoughton in 1986. A mouthful of slang and colloquialisms to mosey around with.

Smaller Slang Dictionary. Compiled by Eric Partridge. First published by Routledge and Kegan Paul in 1961. This book is so full of slang it makes you want to spit.

The Book of Comparisons (or if a flea were the size of a man, how far could it leap?). First published by Sidgwick and Jackson in association with Penguin Books in 1980. This reference book contains drawings, diagrams and charts in order to compare distances, sizes, areas, volumes, masses, weights, temperature, times, speeds, and quantities.

Hand-book of Mottoes. Compiled by C. N. Elvin. First published by Heraldry Today in 1963. True to the last, this book shows them all.

A Dictionary of Mottoes. Compiled by L. G. Pine. First published by Routledge and Kegan Paul in 1983. The complete dictionary of mottoes.

A Dictionary of Catch Phrases. Compiled by Eric Partridge. First published by Routledge and Kegan Paul in 1977. 384 pages.

The Book of Lists. Compiled by David Wallechinsky, Irving Wallace and Amy Wallace. First published by Cassell in 1977. Lists around 300 lists – anything from the ten worst generals to eight cases of spontaneous combustion.

The Guinness Book of Winners and Champions. Compiled by Chris Cook and Anne Mitchell. First published in this form by Windward (W. H. Smith and Sons Ltd), in 1980. Covers the world's natural resources and how man exploits them. Mining, agriculture, fishing, food production, energy, etc., all are explained in an easy to understand way.

Mysteries of the Past. Written by Stuart Holroyd and David Lambert. First published by Aldus Books Ltd, in 1979. Who really discovered America? Many now believe it was not Columbus; this book gives the alternatives. The Egyptian pyramids, Stonehenge, King Arthur's Camelot, and many more mysteries are also examined.

Factfinder. First published by Windward (W. H. Smith and Son Ltd), in 1980. An encyclopaedia of facts and figures, accompanied by more than 300 pictures and diagrams. Subjects covered include: transport, government, communications, people, sport, our world, science, technology, the arts and history.

The Thirty-Six Dramatic Situations. Compiled by Georges Polti. First published in this form by The Writer Inc., in 1977. Already mentioned in Chapter 1, this is a must for all writers of fiction to help with their plotting.

Research For Writers. Written by Ann Hoffmann. First published by A. and C. Black (Publishers) Ltd, in 1975. This goldmine of information sources covers methods of research for all areas of writing from fiction to biography. It shows how to undertake factual and historical research, and how to locate information for both written and pictorial projects. It also includes advice on how to present your work for publication.

Making It Sparkle

You've selected your market, you've found the theme for your piece, now all you have to do is to write it up in as interesting a way as possible. Here are some books to help you give your writing that all elusive sparkle.

The Book of Wit and Humour. Written by Peter Cagney. This edition first published by Thorson Publishers Ltd, in 1976. Contains jokes, jests, wise-cracks, and gags – plus a great deal more. A wealth of ideas to help liven all areas of your writing.

Linda Goodman's Sun Signs. Written by Linda Goodman. First published by Pan Books Ltd, in 1972. The 540 pages of this book provide an in-depth study of the personalities of the different astrological signs. An invaluable aid to characterization.

The Daily Mirror It's a Fact Book. First published by Futura Publications, in 1987. 128 pages of fun-filled facts, from who drinks the most beer to the women who wear C-cup bras.

5,000 One- and Two-Line Jokes (The A–Z of Snappy Sure-Fire Humour on 250 Popular Topics). Written by Leopold Fechtner. First published by Thorsons Publishing Group, in 1979. An invaluable book that can be used as a guide to humorous anecdotes to make your writing come alive.

Quote . . . Unquote 2. Compiled by Nigel Rees. First published in this edition by Unwin Paperbacks in 1982. (First published as *The 'Quote . . . Unquote' Book of Love, Death and the Universe,* by George Allen and Unwin, in 1980.) A compendium of hilarious snippets from 'kings, presidents and menu-writers'.

The Penguin Dictionary of Quotations. Compiled by J. M. and M. J. Cohen. First published in this form by Jonathan Cape in 1962. Originally published by Penguin Books Ltd, in 1960. A volume of 12,000 quotations covering a great many years.

A Dictionary of Contemporary Quotations. Compiled by Jonathan Green. First published by David and Charles in 1982. A collection of some 7000 modern quotations covering a wide area of contemporary life.

Index